THE VALUE IN WORKING WITH NEEDY POPULATIONS

Yolandra A. Plummer, PhD

LifeRich Publishing is a registered trademark of The Reader's Digest Association, Inc.

LifeRich Publishing books may be ordered through booksellers or by contacting:

LifeRich Publishing
1663 Liberty Drive
Bloomington, IN 47403
www.liferichpublishing.com
844-686-9607

Because of the dynamic nature of the Internet, any web addresses or links contained in this book may have changed since publication and may no longer be valid. The views expressed in this work are solely those of the author and do not necessarily reflect the views of the publisher, and the publisher hereby disclaims any responsibility for them.

Any people depicted in stock imagery provided by Getty Images are models, and such images are being used for illustrative purposes only.
Certain stock imagery © Getty Images.

ISBN: 978-1-4897-3799-1 (sc)
ISBN: 978-1-4897-3798-4 (hc)
ISBN: 978-1-4897-3797-7 (e)

Library of Congress Control Number: 2021917592

Print information available on the last page.

LifeRich Publishing rev. date: 08/30/2021

Best Practices in Case Management have changed with
the Pandemic for Low-Income Populations

The COVID-19 pandemic is a game changer for the world in all walks of life including case management. Case managers must follow the guidelines, procedures and policies in place to continue to provide first-rate services to individuals on their caseloads. This is especially important for Case Managers serving low-income populations such as individuals receiving Temporary Assistance for Needy Families (TANF) benefits.

The benefits program is federally funded. The program offers short-term assistance with the goal of helping low-income families to become self-sufficient. The government provides financial assistance, work readiness resources and employment resources. TANF provides a monthly cash stipend which individuals receive on an Electronic Benefit Transfer (EBT) card.

Human services delivery organizations implemented systemic changes to introduce virtual case management systems. This included training staff on virtual platforms, conducting meetings with staff and customers via virtual platforms and investing in virtual technology and/or learning management systems (LMS)

Prior to the pandemic, many Case Managers primarily communicated with the individuals on their caseload in person. Given the mandated safety protocols, Case Managers and other front-line personnel were forced to communicate via telephone and/or email.

Many individuals in low-income households lacked the appropriate technology to conduct regular meetings via virtual platforms such as Microsoft Teams, WebEx and Zoom. This form of communication enabled Case Managers to conduct face-to-face communication with individuals without direct or physical contact, fear of physical proximity and the risk of contracting a deadly disease.

The intent of this article is to examine how case management can be performed during the COVID-19 pandemic and perhaps even afterwards. Structures and patterns have changed now and probably permanently.

Case Managers seeing one or two individuals per day, in person, may be archaic. Driving to and from a customer's home may still be necessary from time to time, but not as much if you are able to see and interact with the customer virtually two or three times a week for 15 to 20 minutes.

The complexity of this equation will require sustain attention and constant tweaking. There will be plenty of trial and error. Virtual technology cannot totally replace the human, physical interaction. Artificial intelligence, no matter how enhanced, cannot remotely replace the nurturing love of a devoted parent. It can, however, be a preferred substitute to an abusive or uncaring guardian than the regular, though perhaps monotonous artificial intelligence.

There are at least three challenges that Case Managers faced during the COVID-19 pandemic. These are the same barriers that other members of society must face and endure, but not in the same amount of time. For instance, the cashier at the grocery store may not know which of the customers checking out items in their line may have tested positive for the Coronavirus. They, however, they have only a relatively short time to interface with that customer before their exchange has ended.

Case Managers, on the other hand, are expected to establish and maintain ongoing rapport with the individuals on their caseload. Though each relationship will be different, they must be fluid and authentic. The Case Manager must maintain a positive and professional relationship with the individuals on their caseload. Over time, each Case Manager develops a relationship where the individual learns to trust them.

Time management poses a challenge in case management. Case Managers often experience high work intensity and reduced autonomy. They conduct daily, weekly, monthly and quarterly meetings as well as daily communication with the individuals on their caseload. During the pandemic, Case Managers must ensure that they are maintaining a quality work/life balance.

Confidentiality and privacy present another challenge in a virtual environment. Case Managers must ensure that individual confidentiality and privacy are maintained on the laptops and computers on which they are documenting case notes. Case Managers must ensure that their computers are free of viruses, password protected and securely stored during the pandemic. Human service agencies must ensure that their agency information and communication systems are secure to prevent any customer breaches of confidentiality.

One of the primary ways Case Managers secure the privacy of individuals is through case documentation. Case documentation should protect individuals' privacy to the extent that it is possible and appropriate. The documentation should only include information that is directly relevant to the delivery of services. The importance of clear, concise and organized case documentation reflects the hallmark of quality case management. Quality documentation ensures accountability, service coordination and improvement for services.

Human services delivery embraces helping other individuals. A third challenge for the Case Manager is being able to sustain a rapport with individuals during the pandemic. Face-to-face contact helps individuals to develop and build relationships. Case Managers serve diverse populations. Strong interpersonal skills help to break down walls with individuals.

These skills help Case Managers to overcome potential barriers they face. Physical and socially distancing have two different meanings in human services. Once a Case Manager connects with the individuals on their caseload, they can build a rapport quickly

Case Managers can conduct home visits virtually. This saves time and transportation costs.

Case Managers must determine the most appropriate use of technology to communicated with individuals on their caseload. There are various communication platforms already in existence including telephone, videoconferencing or other web-based technologies. When a Case manager decides to shift from in-person meetings to a virtual and/or telephonic meeting, the Case Manager must assess the individual's experience and use with and access to each method.

Human services delivery embraces helping other individuals. The third challenge for the Case Manager is being able to build a rapport with individuals. Face-to-face contact helps individuals to develop and build relationships. Case Managers serve diverse populations. Strong interpersonal skills help to break down walls with individuals. These skills help Case Managers to overcome potential barriers they face. Physical and socially distancing have two different meanings in human services. If a Case Manager is able to easily communicate with people and build a rapport quickly, then their interpersonal skills will help break down walls with individuals.

Videoconferencing can offer advantages that telephone operations cannot. Using the videoconferencing enables the Case Manager to have a face-to-face view of the individual. This visual helps the Case Manager to gauge safety or other aspects of the individual's well-being. The videoconferencing can possibly allow the Case Manager to notice interpersonal cues that cannot be obtained from the telephone.

Studies indicate that many low-income households lack broadband Internet access and access to technology. In many instances, the only accessible device in the home for some households is the cell phone.

Additional training must be deployed for both the Case Manager and individual to make the transition successful from the older method to using the newer technologies. Both entities must be trained to utilize the technology appropriately. Low-income households may face barriers to accessing technology. These are challenges that must be conquered.

If telehuman services does become the new norm, it opens more opportunities in human services delivery. It also paves the way for graduate students to learn a new skill and enhance their communication and documentation skills. Increased reliance on telehuman service delivery will provide an opportunity to engage individuals facing greater barriers.

This will enable Case Managers to dedicate more time to identifying interventions to mitigate barriers to their self-sufficiency.

Overview of the PATHS program

The District of Columbia Department of Human Services has a Memorandum of Agreement (MOA) with the University to provide work readiness training to individuals who receive Temporary Assistance for Needy Families (TANF) benefits. The University of the District of Columbia operates the Paving Access Trails to Higher Security (PATHS) program in the School of Business and Public Administration. The program provides UDC to serve as a TANF Employment and Education Program (TEP) provider. The PATHS program provides case management coaching towards education and employment goals. The coaching services are available to parents and caregivers to set goals for their child(ren) and families.

The program also provides training directly tied to career pathways (Contact Tracing, Community Health Worker, Entrepreneurship, Digital Literacy and Microsoft Office) in conjunction with wraparound case management services to address barriers of each assigned participant.

The PATHS wraparound services incorporate a variety of services and resources within the UDC community, District of Columbia government agencies and community-based partners while addressing and responding to individual needs. The PATHS program provides job search and readiness, financial literacy skills, college counseling, life skills, family resources, transportation farecards, access to an onsite clothing boutique and legal assistance for participants seeking records expungement.

Contents

HBCU Trains Contact Tracers in Communities of Color

Yolandra Plummer

School of Business and Public Administration
University of the District of Columbia
yolandra.plummer@udc.edu

ABSTRACT

In June 2020, the University of the District of Columbia began a dual virtual skills certificate program in response to the COVID-19 pandemic. The historically black college and university's (HBCU) introductory program prepared individuals for careers as Contact Tracers and Community Health Workers. A sample of 55 students participated in the pilot program to learn how to investigate the spread of the COVID-19 virus. The program targeted District residents who received Temporary Assistance for Needy Families (TANF) benefits. The TANF program provided work readiness training to low-income families to enable them to move from public assistance to self-sufficiency. Program participants earned a dual certificate in Contact Tracing and Community Health Worker after completing the 20-hour program. The UDC work readiness program created a career pathway in healthcare which combines education, training, credentialing.

The program includes support services to assist individuals with advancing in a high-demand occupation while earning a living wage. The demand for contact training demonstrates that HBCUs are a viable option to engage communities of colors to reduce the transmission of the COVID-19 virus.

Keywords: COVID-19; Contact Tracing; Work Readiness; Historically Black Colleges and Universities (HBCUs); Temporary Assistance for Needy Families (TANF).

Introduction

Nationwide, the COVID-19 pandemic has created an increased demand for Contact Tracers. The University of the District of Columbia (UDC) created a unique program to train students to help increase the District of Columbia's Contact Tracer workforce capacity and expand their infrastructure. The University of the District of Columbia is a public historically black land-grant university, and it is the only public university located in Washington, D.C. The historically black college and university (HBCU) was established in 1851. The University has employed a culturally informed approach to reduce the disproportionate impact of COVID-19 on communities of color. The University of the District of Columbia is one of the few if not only HBCU, that offers free introductory, skills-based workforce readiness training for Contact Tracing.

Tracking the spread of the coronavirus can help reduce the transmission of new infections. This pandemic is responsible for infecting individuals with the disease called COVID-19. [1] In the United States, communities of color have been disproportionately impacted by the pandemic. In the District of Columbia, communities of color are faced with high rates of infections and have been adversely impacted by the COVID-19 pandemic. According to the statistics released by the District of Columbia Executive Office of the Mayor, as of April 23, 2020, 112 out of 139 the lives lost in the nation's capital were African American compared to 15 Caucasians, nine Latinos and three Asians. [2]

Contact Tracers assist in the fight against the pandemic by calling individuals who have been infected by the disease. Contact tracing is a long-used public health tool. It aims to break the chain of transmission of infectious diseases. [3] It is the process of identifying individuals (*also known as contacts*) who have been in proximity with an infected person. Contact Tracing is key to reducing the number of individuals infected by the disease. An expanded public health infrastructure, especially Contact Tracers, will be needed if the infection rate continues to rise.

Crystal Watson, a senior scholar at the Johns Hopkins Center for Health Security warned, "We need to hire up to 100,000 or more individuals to perform this work." According to a report from the Johns Hopkins Center for Health Security, recommended that "Before the United Sates can reopen safely, a new Contact Tracing workforce of at least 100,000 must be in place to trace the contacts of individuals diagnosed with COVID-19. [3]

Contact Tracers face challenges when attempting to communicate with communities of color. Experts recommend that policymakers should engage community members in the development of contact tracing programs. This is especially important when working with low-income communities and communities of color. Individuals in these communities may be suspicious of the health care system, especially as they are facing high rates of infection. Every aspect of a contact tracing program must be examined. [4]

In response to the COVID-19 pandemic, the University of the District of Columbia's Paving Access Trails to Higher Security (PATH)S program introduced the Contact Tracing training in June 2020. The program was created to provide work readiness skills and support services to enable District residents to become self-sufficient. The program aligns directly with the University's mission to serving the needs of the community of the District of Columbia.

Background

The program began in 1997 in response to the Personal Responsibility Work Opportunity Reconciliation Act of 1996 (PRWORA). The legislation is a major welfare reform. President Bill Clinton signed PRWORA into law on August 22, 1996. This fulfilled his 1992 campaign promise to end welfare. [5]

The 1997 law created the Temporary Assistance for Needy Families (TANF) program, which became effective on July 1, 1997 [6]. The TANF program replaced the Aid to Families with Dependent Children (AFDC) program. The AFDC program had been in effect since 1935. It supplanted the Job Opportunities and Basic Skills Training program (JOBS) of 1988. [7] The TANF program was reauthorized in the Deficit Reduction Act of 2005. The University's School of Business and Public Administration (SBPA) oversees the Paving Access Trails to Higher Security (PATHS) workforce readiness program.

Prior to the pandemic, the PATHS program offered in demand and credentialed work readiness training to 700 TANF participants annually. For more than two decades, the PATHS program offered certificate training for a Child Development Associate (CDA), Home Health Aide (HHA), Hospitality and Food Safety Handler. In the last two years, the program expanded its career pathways training to include Concierge Essentials, Property Management, Microsoft Office and Entrepreneurship.

The idea behind a work/career readiness certificate/credential is that potential employees who have achieved a set level of proficiencies in areas needed for entry-level jobs will be provided with a certificate or credential that will signify to employers their level of readiness to be employed. [8]

Creation of Healthcare Career Pathways

The PATHS program offered a virtual skills-based training to 55 students in five cohorts from May to September 2020. The curriculum focused on work readiness behaviors, coaching and vocational training. The training prepares individuals for career pathways in healthcare. The interactive course was taught via Blackboard four days a week.

The PATHS Contact Tracer training is different from other contact tracing programs in several ways. The skills-based training includes a focus on how to communicate with individuals with special needs. According to Dr. Bonnielin Swenor, Director of the Johns Hopkins' Disability Health Research Center, "Communicating with individuals with special needs poses challenges as information is quickly changing". [9]

The PATHS training teaches participants how to identify neighborhood specific resources for individuals who are quarantined and/or in isolation. Program participants can return to obtain refresher training at any time. The program participants represent the communities most impacted by the pandemic. This helps to build trust and a rapport with individuals or contacts.

The University of the District of Columbia offers free virtual skills-based workforce readiness training to District of Columbia residents. Eligible participants must receive TANF benefits in the District of Columbia. The District of Columbia's TANF program provides cash assistance to families in need and supportive services. Families enrolled in the District's TANF program may receive benefits if they are income eligible and have a child in their home. The UDC's PATHS program employs a Two-Generation (2Gen) Approach to serve individuals and families. The approach aims to engage both children and parents collectively. According to the Aspen Institute, the 2Gen approach encompasses the family well-being by engaging both the children and parents together. The PATHS program employs the 2Gen approach as a roadmap to assess a family's needs and barriers. The approach emphasizes education, economic assets and literacy, social capital and health and well-being to create a legacy of economic security that passes from one generation to the next. [10]

Support Services

The PATHS program provides vocational assessments, intensive case management, job coaching towards education and employment goals, skills training and support services. Individuals receive financial assistance to enroll in postsecondary educational program or professional certificate and/or licensing programs. Participants also receive transportation fare cards, uniforms for employment, mental health screenings and access to an onsite clothing boutique.

While these initiatives have not been rigorously evaluated, they aim to increase employment and reduce reliance on TANF benefits. States often provide a range of work supports— intensive case management, rehabilitative services, job coaching and support groups, and referral to other services. [11]

State programs create individual plans geared to helping individuals overcome varied and multiple challenges. The PATHS program creates Individual Responsibility Plans (IRPs) for each participant. The IRP outlines the specific employment goals and work activities and supports for the individual. The IRP identifies support services and barriers that may interfere with the individual's ability to obtain employment. Intensive case management models often connect individuals with mental health counseling, substance abuse treatment, vocational rehabilitation and domestic violence services. [10] The PATHS Case Manager assists the individuals with preparing their IRP.

Work readiness programs help individuals with navigating the array of support services. Instead of having to find their way to each service, hard-to-employ TANF recipients have easier access. [11] The PATHS program assists TANF participants with financial literacy education, childcare referrals, behavioral and/or mental health and substance abuse referrals and domestic violence referrals). Many local offices facilitate program interactions through TANF-funded contracts, formal collaborations, or referrals, though states struggle with integrating services while maintaining a work focus and operating with limited resources.[11] The District of Columbia Department of Human Services contracts with the UDC PATHS program and other TANF Employment Providers (TEP) to administer work readiness services and programs to TANF participants.

An analysis of 20 rigorous evaluations found that work readiness programs boosted employment and earnings about as much for the most disadvantaged recipients as for others. [11]

Barriers

The TANF recipients in the PATHS program faced employment barriers, such as childcare, lack of education, work experience and access to technology. The most common employment barriers TANF recipients face are lack of education or work experience, mental and physical health conditions, work experience and childcare. [12] The training was conducted during the pandemic. Most of the students required childcare. The District of Columbia was under a stay-at-home order. Students were engaged in remote learning. Several participants found it difficult to balance their respective training while managing their child(ren)'s home schedule due to the pandemic.

All the participants possessed a high school diploma or general equivalency degree (GED). Contact Tracers are only required to have a high school degree. Hasak strongly asserts that if an applicant doesn't have a bachelor's degree, their chances of being considered for this in-demand job – especially when compared to other candidates who may have recently became unemployed but have multiple degrees – are very low. He maintains that this exacerbates the inequality of opportunity.[13]

None of the participants possessed previous experience working as an outreach representative, community health worker, in-person assister or navigator. The current job market requires this type of experience for a Contact Tracer. Access to technology was a key barrier. Several families shared school-issued tablets with their children to complete the course. A minimal number of students utilized their cell telephones to participate and complete the course.

Community Needs

According to health equity advocates and community leaders, "there are complex, deeply rooted barriers to engaging people of color in contact tracing efforts, which attempt to find and notify anyone a COVID-positive person has interacted with to stave off community spread". [14] Enlisting **community leaders to promote safety measures** will positively promote the uptake of such behaviors. [15] Contact tracing is critical in communities of color.

"Everyone sees that there's a need to reach pockets of individuals who may not have the same access to information that others do," said Liany Arroyo, Hartford's Health and Human Services Director. [14]

Health proponents declare that the best intentions to promote cultural competency and health equity is not enough to engage communities of color. Decades of substandard health care service delivery and being used as experiments weigh heavily in communities of color. Dr. James Hildreth, President and Chief Executive Officer (CEO) of Meharry Medical College, another HBCU, notes, "The history of abuse at the hands of America's medical establishment, and of misunderstanding rooted in cultural differences, is too long and fraught with missteps". [16]

Pat Baker, President and CEO of CT Health Foundation, a health equity group, asserts that "The health system has a really painful and at times ugly history over how it has treated and experimented on people of color," which is playing and shaping into their consciousness. Baker argues that in communities of color, there is "fundamental distrust" and a "real reluctance to participate" in government health initiatives, including contact tracing efforts that require them to divulge private information. [14]

The PATHS program offers dual certifications in Contact Tracing and Community Health Worker (CHW). Investing in community health workers (CHWs) can help address the social determinants of poor health that disproportionately affect low-income, minority populations and that are magnified during times of crisis. These employees can help improve material conditions, facilitate access to health care systems, and provide psychosocial support. [17]

Community Health Workers (CHW) are trained and trusted members of local communities who share real-world experiences with their neighbors and peers. They are experts in navigating complex systems of care, serving as a link between clinical and community-based services and the people who need them most. [17] The majority of the PATHS program participants reside in Wards 4, 7 and 8 of the District of Columbia. These communities have been most impacted by COVID-19.

Health workers can also enlist the assistance of community leaders—trusted sources of information—to go door to door promoting behavior change. [18] The involvement of trusted community members in promoting social distancing, mask wearing, and quarantining is critical for communities to embrace these behaviors. The PATHS Contact Tracer training program teaches individuals the basics of contact tracing and how to be culturally sensitive to the needs of communities of color while identifying culturally specific resources for individuals.

It is important for Contact Tracers to be aware of cultural sensitivities and assist individuals to navigate the public health systems in which they are employed. Many public health departments are hiring individuals who represent diverse cultural backgrounds and languages to build trust and communication. Fairfax County Government in northern Virginia is recruiting a large number of Community Health Workers. These trained community members understand the specific neighborhood demographics, characteristic and populations that require support. [17]

According to Hasak, policymakers can implement an inclusive Contact Tracing workforce by setting aside a percentage of contact tracing jobs for those Americans who have not enjoyed the benefits of their state's broader economic success. [19] Many individuals from affected communities by the economic downturn possess skillsets that position them to leverage local knowledge, language skills and community capital to perform Contact Tracer jobs.[20] Community organizations offer researchers an entry point into diverse, low-income areas where community members are wary of outside experts. [21] The PATHS program graduates provide skilled capital in communities of color. This is a key asset that will separate them from thousands of individuals in an applicant pool.

The PATHS Contact Tracer program curriculum is led an Epidemiologist, Nurses and other skilled professionals. The curriculum highlights mandated reporting, health information privacy and confidentiality, cultural competency, communicating with individuals with special needs, use of technology, medical terminology, cultural competence, resource identification and critical thinking skills. Many of the students have utilized community-based services and built relationships with these organizations.

Current Gaps

Nationwide, public health agencies are relying on introductory online courses to train entry-level COVID-19 Contact Tracers. This enables state and local agencies to quickly train and certify new Contact Tracers. The training is for individuals interested in entry and mid-level COVID-19 Contact Tracer positions. Individuals do not need to have a public health background to complete the course. The introductory training focuses on building knowledge for remote contact tracing. [22]

According to the National Public Radio (NPR), health experts recommend a minimum of 180,000 Contact Tracers are needed. [23] An expanded public health workforce will help reduce the infectious disease outbreak of COVID-19. Contact tracing requires a dedicated workforce with critical thinking, investigative and people skills. On April 23, 2020, Muriel Bowser, Mayor of the District of Columbia, established the District of Columbia Contact Trace Force to recruit additional Contact Tracers in the District of Columbia. [2]

The Contact Trace Force supports the District of Columbia's Department of Health's critical operation to contain the spread of COVID-19 and prevent hospitalization and death. This is achieved through rapid and robust case identification, case investigation and contact tracing resulting in safe isolation and quarantine for all District residents. This workforce of disease investigators is essential and part of the District's emergency response who operates seven days a week.

In April 2020, the District of Columbia Department of Health employed 65 Contact Tracers. This team initially traced approximately 70% of the confirmed cases in the District of Columbia. [2] The District of Columbia's Department of Health began recruiting a team of 200 Contact Tracers. [2] The beginning salary for a Contact Tracer with the Government of the District of Columbia is $51,000. [24]

In June 2020, the District of Columbia, Guam and the Northern Mariana Islands and seven states (Alaska, Massachusetts, Missouri, New York, Oregon, Vermont and West Virginia) were sufficiently staffed with Contact Tracers. This was based upon their population and COVID-19 rates during a 14-day period. [23]

Universities and Community Colleges have assumed a greater role in Contact Tracer training. At least 20 colleges and universities offer introductory online courses for COVID-19 Contact Tracers. Less than five historically black colleges and universities (HBCUs) offer virtual skills-based training to teach individuals to become Contact Tracers. An opportunity exists for HBCUs to engage impacted communities by providing culturally competent contact tracing training.

William Sutherland maintains that HBCUs are relevant and necessary in 21st Century America. He proclaims, "HBCUS are critical not only for urban America but every community of today and tomorrow's knowledge-based technological society." [24] Hildreth shares a similar sentiment with Sutherland. The Infectious Disease Specialist contends, "HBCUs are uniquely qualified to navigate the long-standing racial divides that have resurfaced amid the pandemic". Hildreth is advocating for HBCUs to provide expanded testing and contact tracing as well as training for a health workforce to meet the "unique needs of vulnerable, low-income of African Americans and underrepresented communities. [16]

Johns Hopkins University, Purdue University Global and the University of Houston are offering free online Contact Tracer classes. [25] Temple University, in Philadelphia, debuted a contact tracing certificate program in June 2020 to its students, health professionals and overall public. [26] While several universities and colleges have created Contact Tracer certificate programs, communities of color continue to mistrust the concept. According to Philip Ricks, PhD, Global Disease Detection Analyst at the Centers for Disease Control (CDC) and Prevention, "An immediate barrier is inherent distrust toward healthcare in communities of color due to experienced biases and mistrust of authority." [27] The PATHS Contact Tracer program offers an inclusive training with cultural humility to establish an effective and safe contact tracing program for communities of color.

Program Description

At the onset of COVID-19, the PATHS program offered workplace readiness skills training and three certificate-training programs from May to September 2020. The PATHS team emailed preliminary training interest surveys to 123 students. Of the 123 students, 55 students responded to the survey and enrolled in the virtual skills training. The workplace readiness skills were included in the training program. These skills are important because they ensure individuals have the basic academic, critical thinking and personal skills necessary to maintain employment. Academic skills such as reading, writing, basic math and communication skills are critical for optimal job performance.

The certificate programs included a dual certification in Community Health Worker and Contact Tracer certification. The other program offerings included the Microsoft Office Specialist and Certified Guest Service Professional certificate programs. There were 54 students who attended the Information Session for the Community Health Worker/ Contact Tracer certification. Twenty-two participants opted to participate in the Microsoft Office Specialist certification.

Findings

All 55 participants enrolled in the dual Community Health Worker and Contact Tracer certification. Thirty-seven individuals enrolled in the work readiness training only. Twelve students enrolled in the Microsoft Office Specialist and 12 students enrolled in the Certified Guest Service Professional.

All 55 students completed the Contact Tracer certification. Forty-three students completed the Community Health Worker certification. Thirty-seven students completed the work readiness training coupled with another training. Twelve students completed the Certified Guest Service

Professional training. Nine students completed the Microsoft Office Specialist.

Technology

Students utilized a combination of cell phones, tablets and/or laptops to participate in the Webex video conferencing and online trainings. Several students shared tablets issued by their child's school.

Enrollment

Forty-eight percent of the participants enrolled in the Community Health Worker and Contact Tracer training programs; thirty-two percent enrolled in the work readiness skills-based training; ten percent of the participants enrolled in the Certified Guest Service Professional training; and ten percent of the participants enrolled in the Microsoft Office Specialist certificate training.

Completion Rates

Thirty-five percent of the students completed the Contact Tracer certification. Twenty-seven percent of the students completed the Community Health Worker training. Twenty-four of the students completed the work readiness skills-based training. Eight percent of the students completed the Certified Guest Service Professional certification. Six percent completed the Microsoft Office Specialist certification.

Employment

Two individuals who participated in the program secured employment as Contact Tracers. This demonstrates a greater need for training opportunities to develop and expand a community-based workforce to promote career pathways and long-term sustainable growth.

Enrollment and Completion Comparison

An examination of the enrollment and completion rates indicates that 55 students enrolled and completed the Contact Tracer certification. All 55 students enrolled in the Community Health Worker training while 43 students completed the Community Health Worker certification.

Thirty-seven students enrolled and completed the work readiness skills training. Twelve students enrolled and completed the Certified Guest Service Professional certification. Twelve (12) students enrolled in the Microsoft Office Specialist certification. Nine students completed this training.

Demographics of the student population:

- Fifty-five participants were female and African American.
- Fifty-four students were heads of households.
- One student represented a two-person headed household.
- One student experienced domestic violence.
- Fifty-five participants required childcare

The initial implementation of the program demonstrated minimal impact for the full student population. There was significant impact in the interest in a healthcare career pathway. This was demonstrated by the number of individuals who enrolled and completed by the Community Health Worker and Contact Tracer training programs.

Conclusion

As District of Columbia policy makers seek to build trust within communities of color, they will need to identify strategies inclusive of the affected communities in contact tracing and public health outreach efforts. The findings demonstrated a strong interest in the Contact Tracer and Community Health Worker certifications. The PATHS workforce efforts have long run services in collaboration with community-based partners. Increased efforts will need to be developed to increase the human capital to better serve communities of color.

The engagement of HBCUs in contact tracing education and outreach may prove to be an equalizer for proactively addressing COVID-19 inequities. "From inception, HBCUs were created out of great social need, and while great social need still persists, today's challenges are different. Today, HBCUs have a great opportunity to redesign the institutions for 21st century sustainability yielding long-term positive outcomes. HBCUs have a huge opportunity to be "catalysts for innovation." [28]

Policymakers will need to make long-term investments in communities that have experienced economic hardships. Community-based training programs provide an opportunity for communities to promote economic recovery. Programs, like the PATHS program, create opportunities for residents to improve their knowledge and skills, earn a living wage and begin a career pathway.

Recommendations

- **Leverage the current human capital built by the University of the District of Columbia's PATHS program to develop a citywide Contact Tracing Corps.** The University of the District of Columbia PATHS program administers a culturally competent curriculum. The PATHS program provides a direct inclusive and equitable pipeline of healthcare professionals and workforce. The citywide Contact Tracer Corps training program would be inclusive of communities of color specifically Wards 4, 7 and 8.

- **The University of the District of Columbia must open its online skills-based Contact Tracer training to all District residents.** As the demand for Contact Tracer staffing increases, there will be a need to train additional individuals and communities. This training must be readily available to meet the growing demand for a public health workforce in affected communities and the public.

- **Expand the current Contact Tracer curriculum**. The University of the District of Columbia must build a curriculum to address the specific needs of the Latinx populations in Ward 4 and African American populations in Wards 7 and 8.

- **The Department of Health should recruit the University of the District of Columbia PATHS Contact Tracers**. The recruitment of individuals who represent communities of color can build a sustainable health outreach employment in affected communities. This will assist individuals in achieving their employment and self-sufficiency goals.

- **Collaborate with public health sororities and fraternities at HBCUs.** The District of Columbia should collaborate with allied health sororities and fraternities at HBCUs to perform community service projects.

- **Partnerships with community-based job training organizations in communities of color**. Training staff at community-based organizations will enable the District of Columbia to develop an inclusive Community Health Worker (CHW) workforce. This is especially important in hotspot areas.

- **Address the barriers** (language, disabilities, financial, etc.) that prevent communities of color from participating in contact tracing efforts to better understand the scope of deaths and confirmed cases, and considerations for providing telehealth services.

- **Educate community-based providers** on how to improve the cultural competencies of their staff.
- **Ensure that all neighborhoods have broadband Internet and adequate neighborhood resources**. The quality of and access to groceries, medical care and housing in neighborhoods East of the River must be improved to ensure that individuals who have tested positive are able to fully quarantine and/or isolate themselves without harming other individuals. Internet connectivity is important for individuals who are communicating with Contact Tracers and medical personnel via telehealth sessions.
- **Create social media messaging**. Focused social media messaging efforts will enable policymakers to communicate dedicated messages to communities of color in the Washington metropolitan area.
- **Public health messaging on public transportation**. The placement of banners with public health messages related to contact tracing on the Washington Metropolitan Area Transportation Authority's (WMATA) buses and subways is a mechanism to engage affected community members.

References

[1] Spectkor, Brandon. Coronavirus: what is 'flattening the curve', and will it work?

LiveScience March 16, 2020. https://www.livescience.com/coronavirus-flatten-the- curve.html.

Accessed on October 20, 2020.

[2] District of Columbia Executive Office of the Mayor. Mayor Bowser establishes coronavirus contact trace force. April 23, 2020.
https://mayor.dc.gov/release/mayor-bowser-establishes-coronavirus-contact-trace-force.
Accessed October 13, 2020.

[3] Watson, Crystal, DrPh, MPH, Cicero, Anita, JD and James Blumenstock, MA and Michael Fraser, PhD, CAE. A national plan to enable comprehensive COVID-19 case finding and contact tracing in the US. April 10, 2020. https://www.centerforhealthsecurity.org/our-work/pubs_archive/pubs-pdfs/2020/200410-_national-plan-to-contact-tracing.pdf.
Johns Hopkins University Center for Health Security. Accessed on October 17, 2020.

[4] Westman, Nicole. Contact tracing programs have to work with local communities to be successful. *The Verge* June 10, 2020.
https://www.theverge.com/2020/6/10/21285166/contact-tracing-community-partnerships-_trust-coronavirus.
Accessed on October 23, 2020.

[5] U.S. Health and Human Services. The Personal Responsibility and Work Opportunity
Reconciliation Act of 1996. Office of the Assistant Secretary for Planning and Evaluation.
September 1, 1996.
https://aspe.hhs.gov/report/personal-responsibility-and-work-opportunity-reconciliation-
act-1996. Accessed on October 27, 2020.
https://aspe.hhs.gov/report/personal-responsibility-and-work-opportunity-reconciliation-
act-1996

[6] Hahn, Heather, Adams, Gina, Spaulding, Shayne and Heller, Caroline. Supporting the
    childcare and workforce development needs of TANF families. The Urban Institute. April
    2016. https://www.urban.org/sites/default/files/publication/79481/ 2000692-Supporting-   the-Child-Care-and-Workforce-Development-Needs-of-TANF-Families.pdf. Accessed on October 22, 2020.

[7] University of Wisconsin, Institute for Research on Poverty. Family Support Act of 1988.
    Focus Spring 1989 https://www.irp.wisc.edu/publications/focus/pdfs/ foc114e.pdf#:~:text=Under%20the%201988%20legislation%2C%20 all%20states%20must%20establish,and%20employment%20 necessary%20to%20avoid%20long-term%20welfare%20dependence. Accessed on October 21, 2020.

[8] LINCs for States. Work readiness credentials.
    https://lincs.ed.gov/lincs/discussions/workplace/07work_ready.html. Accessed on October 29, 2020.

[9] Johns Hopkins University Hub Staff Report. COVID-19 poses unique challenges for
    people with disabilities. *The Hub* April 23, 2020.
    https://hub.jhu.edu/2020/04/23/how- covid-19-affects-people-with-disabilities/.
    Accessed on October 12, 2020.

[10] Ascend at the Aspen Institute. Two-generation approach to leveraging TANF: DC as a case study for policymakers. October 2020.
    file:///C:/Users/antho/Downloads/Two-Generation-Approach-to-Leveraging-TANF_-
    DC-as-a-Case-Study.pdf. Accessed on October 28, 2020.

[11] Bloom, Dan, Loprest, Pamela J. and Zedlewski, Sheila R. TANF recipients with barriers
    to employment. The Urban Institute August 2011.
    https://www.acf.hhs.gov/sites/default/files/opre/barries_employ.pdf.
    Accessed on October 28, 2020.

[12] The Urban Institute. Two generation approach. Metropolitan Housing and Communities
    Policy Center. https://www.urban.org/policy-centers/metropolitan-housing-and-communities-policy-center/projects/host-initiative-action/designing-housing-platform-services/two-generation-approach. Accessed on October 27, 2020.

[13] Zou, Isabella. Can the state convince people of color to trust contact tracing? *The*
    Connecticut Mirror August 11, 2020.
    https://ctmirror.org/2020/08/11/can-the-state-convince-people-of-color-to-trust-contact-tracing/. Accessed on October 16, 2020.

[14] McCarten-Gibbs, Maggie. Building trust to ensure effective and ethical contact tracing in communities of color *Commentary* August 13, 2020.
    https://www.csis.org/analysis/building-trust-ensure-effective-and-ethical-contact-tracing-communities-color. Accessed October 18, 2020.

[15] Farmer, Blake. Meharry President tells Congress to lean on HBCUs in COVID-19 responses. Nashville Public Radio May 27, 2020.
    https://wpln.org/post/meharry-president-tells-congress-to-lean-on-hbcus-in-covid-19-response/. Accessed on October 18, 2020.

[16] Solar O, Irwin A. A conceptual framework for action on the social determinants of health.
    Geneva: World Health Organization, 2010.

https://www.who.int/sdhconference/resources/Conceptualframework foractiononSDH_eng.pdf?ua=1. opens in new tab. Accessed on October 15, 2020.

[17] Landers SJ, Stover GN. Community health workers — practice and promise. Am J Public
Health 2011; 101:2198-2198.

[18] Lehmann, Christine. MA. Contact tracer teams growing amid new challenges. WebMd
Health News June 30, 2020.
https://www.webmd.com/lung/news/20200630/contact-tracer-teams-growing-amid-new- challenges. Accessed October 14, 2020.

[19] Hasak, Jonathan. A diverse approach to scale contact tracing. *Forbes* May 11, 2020.
https://www.forbes.com/sites/gradsoflife/2020/05/11/a-diverse-approach-to-scale- contact-tracing/#375d58994a2b. Accessed on October 19, 2020.

[20] Daube, Elizabeth. An epidemic of inequality. *UCSF Magazine* October 2020.
https://www.ucsf.edu/magazine/covid-inequality. Accessed October 17, 2020.

[21] Association of State and Territorial Health Officials (ASTHO). How to address COVID
19 in communities of color. *ASTHO Blog* June 3, 2020. https://www.astho.org/StatePublicHealth/How-to-Address-COVID-19-in-Communities-of-Color/06-03-20/. Accessed October 17, 2020.

[22] Simmons-Duffin, Selena. June 18, 2020. As states reopen, do they have the workforce they need to stop Coronavirus outbreaks? *NPR: Shots Health* News June 18, 2020. https://www.npr.org/sections/health-shots/2020/06/18/879787448/as-states-reopen-do-they-have-the-workforce-they-need-to-stop-coronavirus-outbreak. Accessed October 17, 2020.

[23] Dempsey, Tom. They can save lives' DC plans to hire hundreds more of Contact Tracer
Force. WUSA News Channel 9. May 1, 2020. https://www.wusa9.com/article/news/health/coronavirus/they-can-save-lives-dc-plans-to-hire-hundreds-more-for-contact-trace-force/65-f2e3bc68-07f1-454a-bebd-dc8b6e7253d3. Accessed on October 22, 2020.

[24] Sutherland, William. HBCUs-relevant and necessary in the 21st century America.
hbcus-relevant-and-necessary-in-21st-century-america. Accessed on October 19, 2020.

[25] Farmer, Blake. Meharry President tells Congress to lean on HBCUs in COVID-19 responses. Nashville Public Radio May 27, 2020.
https://wpln.org/post/meharry-president-tells-congress-to-lean-on-hbcus-in-covid-19-response/. Accessed on October 18, 2020.

[24] Redden, Elizabeth. Teaching contact tracing. *Inside Higher Ed* July 22, 2020.
https://www.insidehighered.com/news/2020/07/22/open-courses-teach-basics-contact-tracing. Accessed on October 22, 2020.

[26] Steinberg, Don. College announces contact tracing certificate program. *CPH News* May 28, 2020.

https://cph.temple.edu/about/news-events/news/college-announces-contact-tracing-certificate-program. Accessed October 15, 2020.

[27] Schroeder, Robert. Contact tracing for communities of color *UIC* July 8, 2020.

https://publichealth.uic.edu/news-stories/contact-tracing-for-communities-of-color/.

Accessed October 19, 2020.

[28] Noel, Marcus. ROI on HBCUs: the role of historically black colleges in the 21st century

Forbes May 2, 2016. https://www.forbes.com/sites/under30network/2016/05/02/roi-on-hbcus-the-role-of-historically-black-colleges-in-the-21st-century/#69785595720b Accessed October 19, 2020.

Telehuman Services Improves the Engagement for Low Income Populations

Abstract

The paper describes a range of evidence-informed strategies that a Historically Black, Colleges and University (HBCU) work readiness program adopted to increase the engagement of Temporary Assistance for Needy Families (TANF) program participants during the COVID-19 pandemic. The program successfully engaged half of the program participants through two-generational (2Gen) approach. The 2Gen approaches target low-income children and parents from the same household and combine parent and child interventions to interrupt the cycle of poverty. These approaches emphasize early childhood education, economic supports, postsecondary education, social capital and health and well-being to create a legacy of economic security. The paper highlights the human services delivery strategies utilized to engage individuals into work readiness training activities during the pandemic. The paper presents data where certain 2Gen activities engaged TANF participants more than other 2Gen activities. The data reveals that half of the participants completed online digital literacy courses and earned training certifications. The intent of the paper is to offer state and local human service agency policymakers' guidance on strategies to increase TANF participant engagement.

Yolandra A. Plummer, PhD

Keywords: TANF engagement, Two-generation (2Gen), Work-readiness, HBCU, COVID-19

1. Introduction

The Temporary Assistance for Needy Families (TANF) block grant provides grants to states, territories and American Indian tribes to finance a wide range of benefits and services for needy families with children. The intent is to ameliorate the effects of economic disadvantage among families with children (Falk and Landers, 2021). The TANF program is more commonly recognized for providing government economic assistance to families and children.

The U.S. Department of Health and Human Services (DHHS) funds the TANF program. Other funded services include childcare, employment and training programs and other social services. Eligible parents are required to complete work and/or activity participation requirements. At the onset of the Coronavirus Disease (COVID-19) pandemic, DHHS modified the work participation requirements in order that participants could focus on the health and safety of their families (Carter, 2020).

As the United States of America faced a national public health and economic emergency, the federal agency granted reasonable cause exceptions to participants that would have faced a penalty for failing to meet the work participation rates due to the COVID-19 emergency. A reasonable cause exception meant that the participant would not incur a financial penalty (*OFA Publishes Guidance on the Implications of the COVID-19 Pandemic for the TANF Program*, 2020)

Examples of the flexibility and good cause exemptions from work requirements included:

- The participant was ill, caring for a child because of daycare and/ or school closures due to the pandemic or worksite and/or training site was closed.
- TANF programs could provide online and/or virtual/remote approaches for participants to engage in work activities virtually. This included online trainings, job search and work readiness programs to encourage and sustain participant engagement; and
- Case Managers were able to perform case management by telephone and other virtual platforms.

2. Statement of the Problem

Prior to the COVID-19 pandemic, the District of Columbia provided services to District residents receiving TANF benefits through its TANF Employment Provider (TEP) program. The TEP programs provided coaching towards education and employment goals. The District of Columbia continued to support TANF participants during the pandemic. This included laptops needed for remote participation.

The TEP programs were responsible for coaching TANF participants to shift their focus to the family's well-being. Once the pandemic began, TEP programs were encouraged to identify strategies to engage TANF participants in health and wellness, early childhood education, postsecondary education, peer network and financial literacy activities. Previously these activities were performed face-to-face. During the pandemic, TANF participants needed to learn how to become engaged using virtual platforms.

3. Relevant Scholarship

The current research on the TANF populations focuses on the government's guidance on work participation rates during the COVID-19 crisis and program instruction on providing case management by telephone and/or other virtual/electronic communication platform (*OFA* Publishes Guidance on the Implications of the COVID-19 Pandemic for the TANF Program, 2020). Research from Benton et. al (2021) examines populations who are best served through virtual services (Benton et al, 2021).

Research from Meyer and Pavetti (2021) documents rigorous evaluations that have demonstrated that well-designed and well-implemented subsidized employment, education, or training programs that focus on building skills and providing adequate support to ensure success can increase the employment and earnings of TANF participants (2021).

This research aims to augment the current body of research on work readiness programs for individuals receiving TANF benefits. This research is an early effort to continue to document preliminary lessons learned by a HBCU to engage traditionally underserved and marginalized populations in work readiness training. It is also an opportunity to identify opportunity gaps between policymakers and communities to embrace collaborative approaches for community problem-solving.

4. An HBCU Engages TANF Participants during the Pandemic

Throughout the COVID-19 pandemic, the University of the District of Columbia's (UDC) Paving Access Trails to Higher Security (PATHS) program placed a major focus on engaging individuals receiving TANF benefits in the District of Columbia. From March 2020 to March 2021, the program staff engaged up to 400 participants in virtual work readiness activities. The diverse group of participants, many who were vulnerable and recognized as a hard-to-reach population, faced multiple barriers to becoming self-sufficient. From March 2020 to March 2021, the UDC PATHS team increased the engagement levels from 32 percent in 2020 to 93 percent in 2021. Several factors contributed to the reversal of engagement levels.

4.1 The PATHS Program

The University of the District of Columbia operates the PATHS program in the School of Business and Public Administration. The training and education program was developed for TANF participants in partnership with the District of Columbia Department of Human Services (DHS). The program provides training directly tied to career pathways in conjunction with wraparound case management services to address barriers of each assigned participant.

Program staff administer a battery of career and literacy assessments to identify needs and strengths that form the basis of the participant's personalized plan of action and offers life skills, financial literacy, job readiness and job search support. The PATHS wraparound services incorporate a variety of services and resources within the UDC community, District of Columbia government agencies and community-based partners while addressing and responding to individual needs. The PATHS program provides life skills, transportation farecards, access to an onsite clothing boutique and legal services for participants seeking records expungement.

4.2 The District of Columbia Department of Human Services

The District of Columbia Department of Human Services, Economic Services Administration is focused on a career pathways approach to workforce development, which connects progressive levels of education, training, support services and credentials for specific occupations in a way that optimizes the progress and success of individuals with varying levels of abilities and needs. The approach works with individuals on long-term planning related to their occupational goals and attainment of self-sufficiency and assists them in meeting financial and family needs while progressing towards those goals (D.C. Department of Human Services, 2020). Career pathways strategies help individuals earn stackable and marketable credentials, engage in further education and employment, and achieve economic success.

The District of Columbia human services agency contracts with the UDC to serve as a TANF Employment and Education Program (TEP) provider. The PATHS program provides case management coaching towards education and employment goals. The coaching services are available to parents and caregivers to set goals for their child (ren) and families.

The District of Columbia Department of Human Services relies on a network of Service Provider partners, and grantees to deliver Education and Occupational Training (EOT), Job Placement (JP), retention services, and family stabilization assistance to non-exempt TANF Customers (D.C. Department of Human Services, 2020).

The mission of the TEP program is to assist TANF participants in enhancing their education and skill levels in preparing for, finding, and retaining unsubsidized employment to ultimately earn family-sustaining incomes and no longer require public assistance. TANF is the central vehicle for helping families who are experiencing economic challenges.

The District human services agency promotes the two-generation model to engage the TANF population. DHS provides cash assistance to individuals and families in need. Families enrolled in the District's TANF program may receive benefits if they are income eligible and have a child in the home. Under the city's TANF program, individuals and families can access to a spectrum of supportive services to meet their needs.

The District's TANF program provides a childcare subsidy to enable parents and/or caregivers to enroll their child(ren) in quality childcare, including before and aftercare. The District of Columbia's Department of Behavioral Health provides counseling to program participants who require access to behavioral and mental health care and substance abuse support. The services are available to individuals and their children.

Tuition assistance is available for TANF program participants.

Individuals are eligible to enroll in post-secondary educational programs or professional certificate and/or licensing programs.

Program participants must meet the following requirements for the TANF program:

- Current resident of the District of Columbia.
- Pregnant or responsible for a child under 19 years of age.
- United States citizen, legal alien and/or permanent resident.
- Meet income requirements based on household size.
- Complete orientation and assessment through the Office of Work Opportunity (OWO); and
- Development of an Individual Responsibility Plan (IRP).

5. Two-Generation (2Gen) Approach

The PATHS Case Managers employed an intentional focus on serving both adults and children together. Case Managers are guided by the Two Generation (2Gen) approach. Two-generation (2Gen) approaches build family well-being, intentionally and simultaneously, by working with children and the adults in their lives together. The approach recognizes that families come in all different shapes and sizes. Families define themselves (What Is 2Gen?, n.d.).

The 2Gen approach is a poverty alleviation strategy that links together five major components in an intensive, sustained strategy to help lifting families out of poverty. The components of a two-generation model include:

- o Early childhood education.
- o Post-secondary education & employment pathways.
- o Health and well-being.
- o Economic assets; and
- o Social capital. (What is 2Gen?, n.d.)

5.1 Coaching and Motivational Interviewing

The PATHS team utilized the 2Gen approach in their case management coaching to support participants in achieving family, educational and employment goals. Case Managers employed motivational, career-coaching techniques to encourage participants to complete education and occupational training programs. The intent was to prepare participants to enter the workforce. Once the Case Manager deemed the participant was prepared to enter a career pathway, the participant should be deemed employable and ready to receive job placement services.

Motivational interviewing gives participants an opportunity to safely explore the advantages and disadvantages of their goals (Sobell and Sobell, 2010). Coaching promotes supportive relationships as participants seek to achieve their goals (Riccio and Wiseman, 2015). TANF programs report participants are more likely to pursue their interests, meet program requirements and obtain desired employment when coaching and motivational interviewing are used.

One of the most compelling rationales for an integrated two-generation approach to service delivery is the multiplier effects for parents and children. Having both parent and child participate in coordinated services should lead to multiplier effects that could not be achieved when parents and children are enrolled in separate and uncoordinated programs.

Spurred on by their children's success, parents may pursue more education and obtain employment that offers a living wage. Further improvement in children's development might follow, for example, in school success and social competence. Ultimately, the benefits of these multiplier effects would accrue not only to the parent or child participating in an intervention, but to the whole family.

6. Creating a Culture of Engagement

The PATHS program employed a combination of participant and organization-focused strategies. The participant-centered strategy utilizes case management to encourage participation (Vu, Anthony and Austin, 2009). The strategy focuses on barriers to employment and other motivational factors that encourage full participation in work-related activities to reduce employment barriers.

Like the participant-focused strategy, the organization-focused strategy supports the goal of employment. The focus, however, is on mobilizing administrative resources to engage participants (Vu, Anthony and Austin, 2009).

6.1 Participant-Focused Strategies

Each new TANF participant receives a telephone call when assigned to the PATHS program. Case Managers invite participants to attend an orientation. During this meeting, the Case Manager will provide an introduction, overview of the PATHS training program and the TANF requirements. The Case Manager will conduct an initial assessment and Individual Responsibility Plan with everyone during the Intake process.

Studies on welfare-to-work programs indicate that successful engagement strategies include a high degree of case management that begins with intake (Freedman et al., 2000). The initial assessment is a one-on-one meeting conducted with the Case Manager. During the meeting, the Case Manager will identify the individual's strengths as well as barriers toward self-sufficiency. Initial assessments are crucial to identify immediate service needs, determine the capacities of participants to work and identify any special needs (Kauff et al., 2004).

Both the TANF participant and Case Manager develop the Individual Responsibility Plan (IRP). The detailed IRP functions as the agreement between the participant, TEP Provider and DHS. It is an agreement developed jointly by the participant and Case Manager. It serves as the participant's roadmap to securing employment and becoming self-sufficient.

The detailed IRP outlines specific steps that the participant consents and commits to taking to address and remove barriers and find and retain employment. It also provides the basis for which any future sanctions would be supported through non-compliance with the IRP on file.

During the initial assessment, the PATHS Case Manager will determine if the participant has any immediate needs, such as food, shelter, medical care, clothing, transportation or childcare. By conducting the initial assessment, Case Managers can identify any immediate needs that might interfere with the individual's participation in work or work-related activities (Vu, Anthony and Austin, 2009). The Case Manager will then provide the participant with the appropriate resources and referrals to address any employment barriers.

6.2 Organization-focused Strategies

The PATHS program used broadly defined and flexible program requirements to increase engagement in program activities during the pandemic. Case Managers encouraged participants to engage in 2Gen and other federally allowable activities such as working or enrolling in an online training course. Participants were given choices of activities that best matched their needs and interests. A range of options can enable participants to identify and find an activity that fits their interests (Vu, Anthony and Austin, 2009).

7. Targeted Telehuman Services Delivery

The PATHS team conducted targeted outreach to each participant via tele human services or virtual human service delivery. Case Managers emailed and/or texted messages to program participants. The tailored message content focused on health and wellness, building social capital, economic security, and financial literacy, early childhood, and postsecondary education. More than 3,000 messages were emailed and/or texted to program participants from March 2020 to March 2021. The outreach included free resources to participants to access virtually and/or in person during the pandemic.

The COVID-19 pandemic disproportionately affected lower income populations (Boserup, McKenney and Elkbuli, 2020). Poverty creates tangible inequities that impact the health, access to education and economic opportunity of people with limited resources (Brenton, 2018). This created an urgency for engaging low-income populations with COVID-19 content and resources (Saul, 2021).

"Low-income populations have some of the lowest levels of adoption of telehealth services, so as healthcare adapts and new innovative care deliver approaches are developed, program staff must ensure the hard-to-reach are included in the shift to virtual care and apply proven strategies for engaging these populations on topics that are important to their health" (McClure, June 19, 2020). Program staff conducted virtual outreach by emailing, calling and texting information about free resources to program participants.

The PATHS team tailored emails and texts to each participant's individual needs. Program staff also conducted virtual meetings with participants via virtual platforms such as Microsoft Teams, Zoom and Facetime.

7.1 Alignment with 2Gen Approaches

The PATHS team aligned their messaging content with the five components of the two-generation approach. Two-generation approaches target low-income children and parents from the same household, combining parent and child interventions to interrupts the cycle of poverty. The two-generation (2Gen) approach builds family well-being intentionally and simultaneously by working in the lives of both children and the adults (What is 2Gen?, n.d.).

Education, economic supports, social capita, and health and well-being transcend from one generation to another to create a legacy of economic security. The underlying intent is to be inclusive, individualized, integrative and impactful in the approach to engagement (National Parent Teacher Association, 2021).

Examples of the 2Gen content delivered to PATHS participants included the following:

Economic Assets- Addressing financial awareness, housing and transportation needs asset building, housing and public supports, financial capacity and transportation.

- o Financial literacy: Free virtual financial literacy and identity fraud courses.
- o Savings: Promotion on opening a College Savings Plan.
- o Housing: Housing education seminar(s); and
- o Obtain documentation: Resources to obtain official government documents.

Health and Well-Being-Behavioral, mental and/or physical health, coverage and access to care, exercise and fitness activities.

- o Fitness class-free scheduled programs that supported healthy lifestyles.
- o Mental health-Mental Health Outreach for Moms (M.O.M.) virtual activities.

and

- o Food pickup sites and locations.

Social Capital-Strengthening family, peer and community networks (connection to other individuals); coaching strategies.

- o Free parenting classes.
- o DHS Parent Café; and
- o Legal matters.

Early Childhood Development-Early childhood development, parenting skills, family literacy and health screenings.

- o DCPS virtual parent meetings and fora.
- o Free virtual Science, Technology, Engineering and Math (STEM) enrichment programs; and
- o College preparation: free virtual college preparation seminars and workshops; Library events:

Free book readings and learning activities.

Postsecondary Education- Access to quality education and clear career pathways.

- o Training tied to a career pathway-UDC Work Readiness training programs

8. Communication and Building Relationships

8.1 Use of Virtual Platforms to Communicate

During the pandemic, the PATHS team utilized alternatives to in-person human services delivery. Team members communicated with participants virtually and remotely. The breakout is as follows:

· Video Platforms (Microsoft Teams, Zoom, etc.)-5%
· Telephone -45%

· Emails-45%
· Texts-5%

8.2 Importance of Respect

The optimal human services delivery begins by promoting a supportive and trusting relationship between providers and participants. In public health, social distancing, also called physical distancing, refers to the practice of keeping space between yourself and others to reduce the chance of contact with those who knowingly or unknowingly carry an illness (Parino, Zino, Porfiri and Rizzo, 2021). Physical distancing does not mean that one cannot practice courteousness and respect.

Raising your own awareness of a participant's time and needs communicates to them that you respect them. Promptly returning phone calls and emails and holding fast to estimated appointment times are practical ways of communicating respect. This shows clients they can rely on you.

The virtual human service delivery improved the communication between PATHS team members and participants. The team connected with participants by building positive relationships with them. Case Managers attempted to share and explain information as clearly as possible to guide participants through their IRPs.

8.3 Use of Data to Track Participation

Case Managers can monitor the work participation status of their caseload on a regular basis. The PATHS Case Managers utilized an electronic database to capture participant participation and engagement rates. This type of monitoring was useful for identifying problems quickly and brainstorming ways to improve the participation rate.

The PATHS team administered targeted case management services to interest participants who were not actively engaged. When these tools are available online, case managers can monitor the work participation status of their caseload on a regular basis (Pavetti et al, 2008).

8.4 Regular Communication

The frequency of the outreach also contributed to the increased engagement. The PATHS team members telephoned, emailed and/or texted two to three times per week. Case Managers conducted follow-up telephone calls after each communication. The preferred choice of communication by both program staff and participants was telephone. Telephone communication was utilized 45% of the time.

Team members emailed participants, at a minimum of 45% of the time, to communicate with participants. Case Managers texted participants 5% of the time. Texting was a secondary communication channel to communicate with participants.

The PATHS team members utilized various methods of verbal, written and virtual platforms to communicate and engage with participants. This included telephone calls, emails, texts, letters and Microsoft Teams and Zoom. The PATHS team established clear communication channels between participants and team members. Participants had access to each team member's email address and telephone number. This provided both the team member and participant with direct access to each other.

8.5 Creating Culturally Diverse Messaging

The messaging content was culturally diverse and specific to the target population served by the PATHS program. The content focused on resources in each of the program participant's neighborhoods and/or which were accessible to participants.

There are potentially smaller and diverse audiences in a "low-income population." This is a decidedly un-monolithic group. The diversity among individuals with low socioeconomic backgrounds is staggering (Brenton, 2018). The PATHS program participants were urban residents of color and/or immigrants and long-time residents dependent on government assistance.

The similarities likely ended there (Brenton, 2018). Each of them had different needs. Each of these subgroups require different strategies and tactics to become self-sufficient. The PATHS team tailored resources to meet each participant's needs and goals as identified in their respective IRPs.

9. Access to Technology

The COVID-19 pandemic compelled the PATHS team to transition to virtual human service delivery options. In-person activities were no longer a reality. Virtual platforms, although used by many, were not an option for all participants. Program participants faced broadband access, hardware (i.e., laptops, tablets or computer) and knowledge deficits. One-third of the students PATHS participants lacked access to technology at home, devices and/or the necessary digital literacy skills.

There were participants with only a smartphone and no data plan There were other participants who had multiple devices and Internet access. This disparity in digital access prompted the PATHS program to partner with DHS and a local community-based program to distribute laptops to participants who did not have a laptop or tablet.

9.1 Digital Inclusion and Equity

According to new research, (Digital Inclusion and Equity: Washington, D.C. Fast Facts, 2021), 55% of households in Ward 7 of Washington, D.C.

do not have broadband Internet access. Fifty-two percent of households in Ward 8 do not have broadband Internet access.

Approximately 37% of PATHS participants reside in Ward 8. A total of 21% of PATHS participants reside in Ward 7.

During the intake process, none of the PATHS participants residing in both Wards 7 and 8 reported a need for broadband Internet access. Less than five percent of participants in both Wards 7 and 8 reported a need for a laptop and/or tablet.

In response, the PATHS developed partnerships to ensure that the underserved population was not excluded from the digital economy. The COVID-19 pandemic presented a barrier for many PATHS participants without access to the Internet or technology. The PATHS program partnered with a community-based organization to obtain laptop devices. DHS also provided laptops for some individuals who did not have a laptop and were interested in improving their digital skills.

To be competitive in the job market, applicants must have digital skills to master the most fundamental basic competencies. COVID-19 was like pouring gasoline on the digital transformation (Ray, 2020). The pandemic ignited the digital transformation and magnified the global workforce. A third of new jobs created in the United States have been in occupations that did not previously exist. It is estimated that 1.1 billion jobs may be transformed by 2030 (Manyika, 2017).

Equitable access to technology refers to all students having access to technology and information regardless of their ethnicity, socio-economic status, age, physical ability or any other quality. Access to technology is not only integral for participants to learn, but also a fundamental component in assisting students with acquiring the knowledge and skills they need to become digitally savvy citizens. A lack of equitable access to technology and information deprives students of learning experiences and can even limit their opportunities, especially after graduation. For many, this inequity was further exacerbated by the virtual learning environment this year (GoGuardian, 2020).

9.2 Digital Literacy

The PATHS team engaged 100 participants to enroll in Digital Literacy and Contact Tracing courses. To function in today's virtual environments, individuals need foundational computer skills to access and consume digital content, create it, and share it. Recent data indicates that as technology evolves, so will the requisite skills needed, and continuing training to remain digitally literate ((Digital Inclusion and Equity: Washington, D.C. Fast Facts, 2021).

Upon completion of the course, students earned three certifications. They included the following certifications:

- Northstar Digital Literacy Essential Computer Skills.
- Northstar Digital Literacy Essential Software Skills; and
- Northstar Digital Literacy Using Technology in Daily Life.

The Northstar Digital Literacy program was utilized to provide the basic skills needed to use a computer and the Internet in daily life, employment and higher education. PATHS participants completed the program remotely. Students learned basic computer and software skills.

Workforce development and digital equity are closely related. One-third of American workers lack the digital skills required for work, school, and life. Access to technology is more than just providing devices and connectivity to students. Access to technology and digital literacy delivers real life impacts on the lives of American workers.

10. Participant Results

10.1 Online Training Certifications

From March 2020 to September 2021, the PATHS program offered online training in Entrepreneurship and certifications for the Community Health Worker and Contact Tracing, and Digital Literacy. The PATHS program offered job-driven training that was directly tied to career pathways. This was important to connect both the TANF and workforce systems. Job-driven training approaches, including career pathways, can provide participants with skills and resources to obtain and retain employment in promising occupations (Administration for Children and Families, 2015).

The virtual classes and human service delivery improved workforce support for PATHS participants. The online courses provided participants with a balanced family and training schedule and increased participant engagement. The online training classes were offered during afterschool hours and provided parents time to focus on their classes.

10.2 Impact of Childcare and Engagement in 2Gen Activities

Previous studies indicated that childcare and transportation were consistent barriers to participant engagement in TANF program activities (Kauff et al., 2004). Childcare referrals plummeted during the pandemic. Parents were able to remain at home and care for their children. Approximately 194 parents, out of 241, engaged in early childhood activities for and with their children.

PATHS program participants engaged in the following 2Gen activities:

- Early Childhood Education-66% (194 individuals).
- Economic assets - 4% (12 individuals).
- Health and wellness - 28% (75 individuals).

- Postsecondary education - 11% (33 individuals); and
- GED/High school diploma - 6% (19 individuals)

10.3 Engagement in Postsecondary Education

A total of 33 individuals enrolled in five different institutions of higher learning to advance their education. There were 75 participants engaged in health and wellness activities. Nineteen individuals completed and/or earned high school diploma and/or general equivalency degree (GED).

10.4 Program Demographics

Approximately 95% of the PATHS participants were female and African American. Most of the PATHS participants represented single-headed households. Fifty percent of the PATHS participants resided in Wards 7 (21%) and Ward 8 (37%) of Washington, D.C. None of the PATHS participants residing in Ward 7 reported a lack of broadband Internet access.

Less than 10 PATHS participants in Ward 7 reported a lack of access to a laptop and/or tablet. According to the Census, 26.3% of the population in Ward 7 lives below the poverty line. The median household income in Ward 7 is $45,318. This is about half of the amount of the medium household income in the District of Columbia $86,420. 85.8% of the residents in Ward 7 have graduated from high school or higher (Ward 7, DC Profile Data, 2019).

Of the 37% of PATHS participants residing in Ward 8, all have reported having broadband Internet access. Less than 10 reported a need for a laptop and/or tablet.

According to the Census, 32.9% of the population in Ward 8 lives below the poverty line. The median household income in Ward 8 is $35,245. This is nearly two-fifths of the median household income in

Washington, D.C. 86.% of the residents in Ward 8 have graduated from high school or higher (Ward 8, DC Profile Data, 2019).

At the beginning of the pandemic, many TANF participants, largely female, faced barriers to employment, including low-wages, lack of affordable childcare, COVID and skills deficits. As employers seek to resume business as usual, many are facing labor shortages. Despite the unemployment numbers being in the millions, there are 8.1 million vacancies (Filipovic, 2021). The vacancies are highly concentrated among America's low-wage workforce. The key industries include restaurants, warehouses, manufacturers and services. Now is the time for employers to consider the TANF population as a viable pool to fill the vacancies. Employers will need to consider additional flexible work schedules, on-the-job training and virtual employment opportunities to recruit and address workforce shortages.

11. Lessons Learned

As the world faces the 'new normal' post-COVID, there are important lessons that should be implemented post pandemic to engage the TANF population.

1. Historically black colleges and universities (HBCUs) must collaborate to serve our most vulnerable populations.
2. Human service agencies must prioritize training on culturally competent care. Community health workers can serve as a resource to assist participants in navigating the human services delivery system.
3. Community-based organizations can assist Case Managers with building relationships and trust through advisory councils, or community board memberships.

4. It is essential that agencies continue to engage individuals online and by telephone, to address their critical needs.

5. The delivery of tele human services reduced travel time, childcare costs and time and reduced barriers to services for parenting support. The virtual human service delivery will continue to provide benefits to both employers and vulnerable populations.

6. As technology continues to reshape the economies around the world, individuals must acquire the new digital skills to transform themselves in the new digital reality.

7. COVID-19 has increased the awareness for the need for digital skills for all industries.

   Technology touches every employee now. "Every job is in some way a digital job," agrees Naria

   Santa Lucia, Microsoft Philanthropies' General Manager of employability skills. "Even if you're

   not working in the tech sector, everyone needs to have the basics of digital fluency (Ray, 2020)."

8. Hard-to-employ and underemployed parents are a viable option for businesses with growing workforce shortages to sustain economic growth and competitiveness.

9. States must examine industry workforce needs to encourage TANF participants to pursue a sustainable career pathway and build a stronger economy

References

Administration for Children and Families. (2015). Systems to Family Stability National Policy Academy Overview. U.S. Department of Health and Human Services. https://www.acf.hhs.gov/sites/default/files/documents/ofa/systems_to_family_stability_academy_overview.pdf

Benton, A., Tschantz, J., Vandenburg, A., Waters, A., & Winston, P. (2021, February). Virtual Human Services for Different Populations. U.S. Department of Health and Human Services Office of the Assistant Secretary for Planning and Evaluation. https://aspe.hhs. gov/sites/default/files/migrated_legacy_files/199061/VHS-Different-Populations.pdf#:~:text=While%20virtual%20human%20services%20 thus%20offer%20a%20range,urban%20area%20that%20lacks%20 accommodate%20with%20virtual%20visits.

Boserup, B., McKenney, M., & Elkbuli, A. (2020). Disproportional impact of COVID-19 pandemic on racial and ethnic minorities. American Surgeon, 86(12), 1615– –1622. https://doi.org/10.1177/0003134820973356

Brenton, K. (2018, November 12). Improving outreach to low-income populations. SE2 Communications. https://se2changeforgood. com/2018/11/12/improving-outreach-to-low-income-populations/

Carter, C. (2020, July 22). Temporary Assistance for Needy Families Program Instruction. U.S. Department of Health and Human Services Administration for Children and Families

Office of Family Assistance. https://www.hhs.gov/guidance/sites/ default/files/hhs-guidance-documents//tanf_program_instsruction_ final722202.pdf

Digital inclusion and equity: Washington, D.C. fast facts. (2021). Center for Nonprofit Housing and Economic Development. https://cnhed.org/wp-content/uploads/2021/05/Digital-Inclusion-and-Equity-One-Pager1.pdf

District of Columbia Department of Human Services. (n.d.). TANF for District Families. D.C. Department of Human Services. Retrieved June 4, 2021, from https://dhs.dc.gov/service/tanf-district-families

District of Columbia Department of Human Services. (2020). D. C. Department of Human Services (DHS) Primary and Secondary Service Provider Manual. D.C. Department of Human Services.

Falk, G., & Landers, P. (2021, March). Temporary Assistance for Needy Families and ProposednCOVID-19 Pandemic Economic Relief: In Brief. Congressional Research Service.

https://crsreports.congress.gov/product/pdf/R/R46692

Filipovic, J. (2021, June 2). *The real reason employers cannot hire enough workers.* CNN.

https://www.cnn.com/2021/06/01/opinions/covid-workers-labor-shortage-pandemic-benefits-filipovic/index.html

Freedman, S., Friedlander, D., Hamilton, G., Rock, J., Mitchell, M., & Nudelman, J. (2000, June). *National Evaluation of Welfare-to-Work Strategies: Evaluating Alternative Welfare-to-Work Approaches: Two-Year Impacts for Eleven Programs: Executive Summary.*

Manpower Demonstration Research Corporation. https://aspe.hhs.gov/reports/national-evaluation-welfare-work-strategies-evaluating-alternative-welfare-work-approaches-two-year

GoGuardian. (2020, September 2). *What it means to have equitable access to technology for today's students and educators.* https://www.goguardian.com/blog/technology/equitable-access-to-technology/#:~:text=Equitable%20access%20to%20technology%20refers%20to%20all%20students,status%2C%20age%2C%20physical%20ability%2C%20or%20any%20other%20quality

Kauff, J., Derr, M. K., & Pavetti, L. (2004, August). *A study of work participation and full engagement strategies*. Mathematica Policy Research, Inc.

https://aspe.hhs.gov/reports/study-work-participation-full-engagement-strategies-1

Manyika, J. (2017, May). *Technology, jobs and the future of work*. McKinsey Global Institute.

https://www.mckinsey.com/featured-insights/employment-and-growth/technology-jobs-and-the-future-of-work

McClure, B. (2020, June 19). *The importance of tailored telehealth engagement for low-income populations*. MPulse Mobile.

https://mpulsemobile.com/2020/06/the-importance tailored-telehealth-engagement-for-low income-populations/

Meyer, L., & Pavetti, L. (2021, January). *TANF Improvements Needed to Help Parents Find Better Work and Benefit from an Equitable Recovery*. Center for Budget and Policy

Priorities. https://www.cbpp.org/research/family-income-support/tanf-improvements-needed to-help-parents-find-better-work-and

National Parent Teacher Association. (2021, June 1). *Tools to Turn Your Commitment to*

Diversity, Equity & Inclusion into Action [Video]. YouTube.

https://www.youtube.com/watch?v=5RBOvxcsq-Y

OFA publishes guidance on the implications of the COVID-19 pandemic for the TANF program. (2020, March 24). U.S. Department of Health and Human Services Administration for Children and Families. https://www.acf.hhs.gov/ofa/news/ofa-publishes-guidance-implications-covid-19-pandemic-tanf-program

Parino, F., Zino, L., Porfiri, M., & Rizzo, A. (2021). Modelling and predicting the effect of social distancing and travel restrictions on COVID-19 spreading. *Journal of the Royal Society*

Interface, 18(175), 1–10. https://doi.org/10.1098/rsif.2020.0875

Pavetti, L., Kauff, J., Derr, M., Maxx, J., Person, A., & Kirby, G. (2008, December).

Strategies for increasing TANF work participation rates (No. 5). Mathematica Policy

Research, Inc.

https://aspe.hhs.gov/reports/strategies-increasing-tanf-work-participation-rates-summary-report-0

Ray, S. (2020, November 16). *Free online digital skills courses revive hope and careers for millions amid the pandemic.* Microsoft.

https://news.microsoft.com/features/free-online-digital-skills-courses-revive-hope-and-careers-for-millions-amid-the-pandemic/

Riccio, J., & Wiseman, M. (2015, November). *The "FSS-X" demonstration: Combining an executive skills coaching model with financial incentives to improve economic mobility for families with housing subsidies See more at: https://selfsufficiencyresearch.org/content/fss-x-demonstration-combining-executive-skills-coaching-model-financial-incentives-improve*

(Corporation, Ed.). Manpower Demonstration Research Corporation.

Saul, A. (2021, April 2). *Outreach to vulnerable populations during the COVID-19 pandemic.*

Social Security Administration.

https://blog.ssa.gov/outreach-to-vulnerable-populations-during-the-covid-19-pandemic/

Sobell, L. C., & Sobell, M. (2008). *Motivational interviewing strategies and techniques:*

Rationales and examples. Nova Southeastern University.

https://www.esrdnetwork.org/sites/default/files/MI_rationale_techniques.pdf

Targeted communication: The key to effective stakeholder engagement. (2016). *Procedia*

-Social and Behavioral Sciences, 226, 431–438. https://doi.org/10.1016/j.sbspro.2016.06.208

Vu, C., Anthony, E. K., & Austin, M. J. (2018). Strategies for engaging adults in welfare-to-work activities. *Families in Society: The Journal of Contemporary Social Services, 90*(4),

359–366. https://doi.org/10.1606/1044-3894.3929

Ward 7, DC Profile data. (2019). Census Reporter. https://censusreporter.org/profiles/61000US11007-ward-7-dc/

Ward 8, DC Profile data. (2019). Census Reporter. https://censusreporter.org/profiles/61000US11008-ward-8-dc/

What is 2Gen? (n.d.). Ascend at the Aspen Institute. Retrieved March 20, 2020, from

https://ascend.aspeninstitute.org/two-generation/what-is-2gen/

The District of Columbia Government TANF Program: A Successful Welfare-to-Work Program (A Case Study of inter-departmental Collaboration at the University of the District of Columbia)

Abstract

This paper describes the collaborative partnership between the University of the District of Columbia and the local government's human services agency. The government entered into a partnership with the university to provide job skills training to District residents receiving Temporary Assistance for Needy Families (TANF) benefits. Through the collaboration, the government has been able to prepare individuals for employment and become self-sufficient.

The University has engaged faculty in interdisciplinary collaboration and professional development. This partnership provides a snapshot of the value of the university in serving both the residents of the District of Columbia and local government policymakers.

Yolandra A. Plummer, PhD

Yolandra Plummer, PhD, is an associate professor at the University of the District of Columbia (UDC) in the School of Business and Public Administration (SBPA), Department of Public Administration. She also serves as the Director of the SBPA's Institute of Human Services Delivery. Dr. Plummer also serves on the Executive Board of Quality Trust for Individuals with Disabilities. She previously served as the Chief of Staff at the Department on Disability Services (DDS).

Introduction

Most government programs cannot meet all the needs of all its population. In response, policymakers engage in collaboration to circumvent bureaucratic boundaries and red tape. Today's human service delivery system includes a number of human service agencies that operate independently of each other. Often, each agency works in silos and is unaware of whom the other is serving. At times, more than one agency may be competing for the same resources and duplicating services. This creates a system of fragmented services. The end result is an unmet need, that of a low-income family.

This fragmentation presents insurmountable barriers for participants with multiple needs (Edelman & Radlin, 1991). Increasingly government agencies are collaborating with colleges and universities to administer public services and goods. In particular, human service agencies collaborate with universities to promote self-sufficiency and offer a unified service delivery system. Local governments collaborate with local colleges and universities to develop programs to serve their target populations.

The University of the District of Columbia is a public, historically black college and university (HBCU) and land grant institution in the District of Columbia. The University's mission is to offer an affordable education and workplace learning opportunities. The University partners with the local human services agency to provide job skills training to individuals receiving Temporary Assistance for Needy Families (TANF) benefits.

This collaborative partnership is consistent with the university's mission and vision. The university seeks to establish pathways for matriculation from workforce development. The vision also seeks to align educational offerings to student interests and District of Columbia priorities.

This article will examine how one government jurisdiction collaborated with a local university to provide services to residents. The research will draw upon the literature that focuses on the infrastructure and systems to support collaboration between local governments and university from the academic perspective.

Background

The Personal Responsibility and Work Opportunity Reconciliation Act (PRWORA) of 1996 changed the nation's welfare system. The federal legislation (Public Law 104-193) was introduced by Representative Eugene Clay Shaw, Jr. (R-FL.22). President Bill Clinton signed the Act into law on August 22, 1996. The Personal Responsibility and Work Reconciliation Act replaced the Temporary Assistance for Needy Families (TANF) benefits program. The new legislation became effective on July 1, 1997. The legislation replaced Aid to Families with Dependent Children

(AFDC), the federal entitlement program for low-income families, with state administered block grants.

The federal entitlement program had been in effect since 1935. In 1997, the TANF Program replaced the Job Opportunities and Basic Skills (JOBS) training program of 1988. The TANF program was reauthorized in the Budget Deficit Reduction Act of 2005. The Job Opportunities and Basic Skills Training program (JOBS) was a welfare-to-work program created by the Family Support Act of 1988. he Family Support Act replaced the Work Incentive program (WIN) created by the Social Security Act Amendments of 1967 (Hagen and Lurie, 1993 and Reid and Smith, 1972). The Family Support Act put the program under titles IV-A and IV-F of the Social Security Act.

The Temporary Cash Assistance for Needy Families (TANF) is a benefit program that provides cash assistance to needy families with dependent children when available resources do not fully address the family's need. Program participants are prepared for independence through job skills training, work activities and employment.

The legislation pushed states to experiment by designing their own social welfare programs. Though the legislation imposed new requirements on the state use of federal welfare funds, each state was encouraged to independently configure their program (Moffitt and Ver Ploeg, 1999).

In order to qualify for the TANF program in the District of Columbia, an individual must be a resident of the District of Columbia, pregnant or responsible for a child under 19 years of age. Other qualifications may include being a U.S. national, citizen, legal alien, or permanent resident with a low or very low income and be either under-employed (working for very low wages), unemployed or about to become unemployed (D.C. Department of Human Services (DHS), Economic Security Administration (ESA), 2014). Approximately 17,000 District of Columbia residents receive TANF benefits (DC Action for Children, 2016).

The University of the District of Columbia is a public, historically black college and university (HBCU) and land grant institution in the District of Columbia. The University's mission is to offer an affordable education and workplace learning opportunities. The partnership is consistent with the university's mission and vision. The University seeks to establish pathways for matriculation from workforce development. The vision also seeks to align educational offerings to student interests and District of Columbia priorities.

Institutions of higher education have vested interests in building strong relationships with surrounding communities of their campuses. They do not have the option of relocating and are of necessity place-based anchors. While businesses and residents often flee urban areas, universities remain (Birch, Perry and Taylor, 2013). Leaders have called for "engaged colleges and universities." Such an institution systematically structures, rewards and encourages partnerships and collaborations. An engaged institution collaborates with communities, not only in the traditional sense of educating students and producing relevant research, but also by focusing on community partnerships and collaborations (Mattessich, 1992). The University's current partnership with the government of the District of Columbia demonstrates its commitment, as an anchor institution, to serving the residents of the District of Columbia. Furthermore, it is the beginning to developing future collaborative agreements to address the needs of targeted populations.

A Collaboration Formed

In the District of Columbia, the Government of the District of Columbia human service agency administers the TANF benefits program. In 1996, the Department of Human Services entered into an agreement with the University of the District of Columbia (UDC) School of Business and Public Administration (SBPA). The School of Business and Public Administration's Institute of Human Service Delivery administers the job skills training program for TANF customers. The purpose of the program is to engage and train District residents who were receiving benefits in order to become self-sufficient and employable.

The agreement outlines three key goals. The first is to create a job skills training program for 700 low-income residents receiving Temporary Assistance for Needy Families (TANF)-*formerly known as the Aid to Families of Dependent Children* (AFDC). Second, to provide technical assistance to the Department of Human Services (DHS), Economic Security Administration (ESA) staff. Finally, to sponsor an Annual Capacity Building and Technical Assistance symposium for DHS grantees and community-based partners.

The collaboration reflects a growing trend of government and municipalities partnering across campuses to create sustainable urban partnerships.

In the mid to late 1980s, the Department of Human Services (DHS) was the largest District agency. It operated the city's largest budget and employee population. The agency had oversight over the city's entire health and human services delivery system. At the time, this included childcare, adult education, health care, welfare reform, elder care and other public services.

The demand for expanded capacity and greater efficiency led to the restructuring of the agency. The human services agency now primarily focuses on the human service delivery system for residents.

Since 1996, the Institute of Human Service Delivery has been working to improve the well-being of low-income individuals and families in the District of Columbia. The center is a component of the University of the District of Columbia (UDC) School of Business and Public Administration (SBPA). The center is located within the university's School of Business and Public Administration. The Institute's programs serve District residents who receive Temporary Assistance for Needy Families (TANF) benefits under the state TANF block grant.

The Institute, along with six other community-based providers, serves as TANF Employment Program (TEP) providers. The Institute offers two programs for residents receiving TANF benefits. The first program is the Paving Access Trails to Higher Security (PATHS). This program provides life skills training, job search and readiness training, vocational assessments, transportation assistance and job skills training. The job skills training includes certified nursing assistant (CNA), home health aide (HHA), hospitality, computer skills training, entrepreneurship and child development associate (CDA).

The second program, Program on Work, Employment and Responsibility (POWER), is for individuals receiving TANF benefits as well. The POWER Program offers specialized services and resources to DC residents with disabilities who are receiving TANF benefits.

Individuals who are in the POWER program are exempt from work participation requirements (but must comply with their self-sufficiency plan). Customers in the POWER program are exemption from the 60-month TANF time limit. The amount of a customer's cash assistance to the benefit amount received before any reductions (in the event, the customer, has exceeded the 60-month TANF time limit). The POWER program team engages customers through health and wellness promotion activities. The team also assists customers with obtaining Social Security Income. The University of the District of Columbia (UDC) team helps offer these services. The Institute also provides professional development training for local government staff and representatives of community-based grantee organizations. The Institute's programs promote workforce development, life skills training and health education at the community level.

Collaboration Begins at Home

Both the District of Columbia and University have mutually benefitted from the partnership. Together, both entities were able to create effective solutions to community needs, expand implement best practices and increase the understanding of human service delivery systems in urban settings. The University offers an environment whereby, both faculty and students, to foster an ethic of service and civic participation. Faculty and students gain experiential learning and professional development training.

This partnership is an opportunity for the University to examine its ability to identify and support new partnerships. The funding for university partnerships is important because of: 1) It can provide initial funding for programs and potentially attract funding from other sources in the future and 2) enable universities to develop and sustain an effective infrastructure and/or conducive environment to engage with communities (Ashenden et al., 2011).

The resources required to create the 'infrastructure' to support the program may be overlooked. The Institute is a single partnership. A significant proportion of these costs are for academic and administrative support staff time, although there may also be marketing and promotion costs as well as general office-related overheads. Faculty and staff are paid additional pay during the summer to perform work with the program. The Institute provides two computer labs, contracts with vendors to provide direct services and pays educational and examination fees. Additional costs include marketing and promotional materials for training, workshops and conferences, uniforms and other related costs for the program participants

If a University seeks status as an engaged institution-an institution that through its place-based relations strengthens its role as an urban anchor institution-then this must be registered in the institution's fiscal and structural investment in the process (Birch, Perry, Taylor, 2013).

The physical geographical location of the University has promoted intra university collaboration also has a geographical dimension. The majority of the services for program participants are offered at the University's main campus. The Institute provides the majority of its core services onsite at the university. This includes case management, job search and readiness training, intake and assessment, transportation assistance, child care referrals, health care coordination, mental health screenings and job skills trainings.

Ancillary supports services, such as vocational assessments, health and wellness support groups, life skills training, job search and readiness are offered at the main campus as well. Coordination of these services are centralized and managed through the SBPA Institute. A few of the job skill training classes are offered one of the University's other campus locations. One of the most unique features of this initiative has been its ability to utilize intra university collaboration. The across-university collaboration has been effective in improving the sustainability of the program because the majority of the services are offered at one location. Key questions for the program point to whether intra university collaboration will continue to yield benefits to the university-government partnership, enhance the support mechanisms for the program and influence the likely sustainability of support mechanisms and partnerships.

Universities are increasingly supportive of focusing on collaboration between researchers who offer different and complementary perspectives, knowledge, experience and skills that can result in innovative approaches to problem solving (Office of Responsible Conduct of Research, 2005). The program currently participates in intra university collaborations with the Departments of Social Work, Counseling and Psychology and Nursing.

Social Work

Since the beginning of welfare reform, the National Association of Social Workers (NASW) have supported PRWORA. The organization's core values include social justice and belief in the dignity and worth of each person. The organization's members maintain that the TANF program must accommodate the needs of all families, particularly those with disabilities.

According to the National Association of Social Workers, there is a distinct lack of awareness regarding the high percentage of families on TANF that are coping with disabling conditions. The most common disabilities for TANF beneficiaries include physical or mental health problems, drug and alcohol addictions, developmental disabilities and responsibility for the care of a disabled family member. Many are coping with one or more chronic conditions.

The General Accounting Office (GAO) found that at least 44 percent of TANF customers have physical or mental impairments or are caring for a child with impairments, compared with 15 percent of the non-TANF population (2002). Figures around 50 percent, both higher and lower, have been confirmed by the U.S. Department of Health and Human Services' Inspector General, as well as The Urban Institute, the Manpower Demonstration Research Corporation (MDRC) and others.

The Institute's program enlists the assistance of the University's licensed social workers and clinicians to conduct mental health and vocational assessments. The clinicians conduct screening and assessment procedures. These tools help identify the family's barriers and steps needed to assist them with obtaining greater independence.

The Institute employs Case Managers to advocate and guide the program participants. With the advent of the 1996 welfare reforms, the roles and responsibilities of the job changed dramatically. Case Managers hired prior to 1996 to work on the front lines in human services were trained to assess participant eligibility by processing them to determine their income and expenses, according to Cynthia Woodside, senior government relations associate at the NASW.

According to Woodside, "They were no longer just checking to determine whether someone was eligible for the program, but were really charged with screening for barriers, helping people find jobs and being a job coach once they found one." She adds "The workforce was not sufficiently trained to take on these responsibilities, and they recognized this fact." Many of the Institute's Case Managers were not prepared for the challenges of serving the TANF population.

The University's faculty in the Department of Social Work provided training for frontline staff on how to identify the basic signs and symptoms of the more common mental health disorders and substance abuse problems. If problems were identified, then one of the University's clinician's would provide a more in-depth assessment. Ensuring a qualified, stable and professional TANF workforce is a critical component of the program. Following enactment of the PRWORA, employees whose primary task had been to determine client eligibility was suddenly called upon to conduct customer assessments, engage customers in job search and job readiness training and placement activities, make referrals to related programs and special services and track customer activities. Many states have not invested sufficiently in the training needed to prepare their Case Managers for these additional tasks, nor have they hired more highly skilled staff.

Social workers are trained professionals who have bachelors, masters, or doctoral degrees in social work from an accredited social work program. In contrast, the majority of Case Managers today have little to no professional social work training. Case Managers often possess college degrees, but typically in fields unrelated to social service delivery. Some states only require Case Managers to have a high school diploma. Case Managers with the Institute possess a Masters degree along with at least one year of professional case management experience. They receive continuous training. This includes, but not limited to, mandated reporter writing, case management documentation, SSI/SSDI Outreach, Access and Recovery (SOAR), screen co-occurring disorders, non-crisis prevention intervention and domestic violence.

The ultimate success of welfare reauthorization depends, in large part, on the skills and abilities of the TANF workforce to implement the policies, it is critical that resources be directed to address current shortcomings.

Counseling and Psychology

The transition from welfare to work poses challenges. Individuals may face mental health issues and/or contextual variables (i.e., lack of a well-paying job). The Institute engages both Department of Counseling and Psychology faculty and students as consultants and interns. Faculty provide vocational guidance and psychological testing. The faculty maintains strong relationships with local mental health agencies and organizations in an effort to serve the needs of the Institute's participants.

Collaboration is drawn from many fields.,including social work, public adminsitration and sociology and others (Lasker and Weiss, 2003). Licensed clinicians and graduate students conduct vocational assessments and provide vocational guidance to participants seeking to transition from welfare to work.

Nursing

University nurse faculty conduct training workshops for the Institute's Case Managers. This includes reviewing medical records, developing comprehensive and coordinated physical and health care plans and record keeping. Specifically, the nurses demonstrate how to develop medical summary sheets for customer records. Case Managers are also trained on how to document and report health barriers in the centralized reporting system. Nurse faculty also receive continuous education units (CEUs) for training and use them as a part of their professional portfolios.

Yolandra A. Plummer, PhD

Collaborative Education begins Early

The Institute offers internships to a broad mix of students enrolled in the Counseling and Psychology, Public Administration, Social Work and Computer Information Systems. The program includes students from other universities in the metropolitan area as well. Students must begin working together before they actually start working. Students participate in a year-long internships and collaborate with Case Managers in the development of each participant's development plan. Students gain from the experiences and learn to distinguish and differentiate certain conditions (i.e., depression, anxiety) from poorly defined vocational interests and lack of job-related self-efficacy (Edwards, et. al, 1999).

Students are taught consultation, program development and program evaluation skills through work with social service agencies. The provision of such experiences will likely advance the training agenda of the field (Edwards et. al, 1999).

Many professionals operate in silos. It is incumbent upon universities and training programs to expand interdisciplinary educational opportunities and programs to help foster collaboration among students before they enter the workforce (Robert Wood Foundation, 2010). Interdisciplinary collaboration can provide people with many learning experiences, but only if they are properly managed (Chu, 2013).

Lessons Learned

Through the collaboration, the University has trained more than 10,000 District residents receiving TANF benefits and prepared them to work in hospitality and health careers. The University has opened and shared its core facilities with government officials. Through the Institute, the University has provided onsite leadership, sponsored and conference for more than 15 community-based organizations on an annual basis and continuously developed professional development workshops training for the human services front line staff.

Furthermore, the University has hired five of its interns who remain as current employees, formed community partnerships and increased its grant funding from the government. This has increased the visibility of the program and confidence of the District government in the University's ability to provide and sustain city programs.

There are scholars who are cautious about interdisciplinary collaborations in the academic setting. For some, concerns included credit for publishing (Chu, 2013). Others maintain that the focus on interdisciplinary research distracts one from their primary field of study.

As the District government policymakers juggle competing priorities and dwindling budgets, they must evaluate the value of university partnerships. Universities can share training and technological resources with government to reduce their agency cost. Both entities share common interests and objectives in serving the District of Columbia. Moving forward, both entities must evaluate innovative approaches to service delivery, including best practices to promote government and university collaboration.

Works Cited

"The Engaged University," (Spring /Summer 1998). *Penn State Outreach* 1, no. 1

Ashenden, Stuart, Hoult, Elizabeth, Matthews, Nairne, Bruce, Steve and Pratt, Jonathan. (2011). Collaboration between Universities: An Effective Way of Sustaining Community University Partnerships?" *Gateways: International Journal of Community Research and Engagement Vol 4: 119–35.*

Birch, Perry and Taylor, 2013. "Universities as Anchor Institutions," *Journal of Higher Education Outreach and Engagement,* v. 17, no. 3. 7-15.

Chu. Andrea. (2013). "Interdisciplinary Collaboration at the University Level," Honors Research Thesis. Ohio State University: School of Environment and Natural Resources.

Edwards, Scott, Rachal, Chris and Dixon David N. (1999). "Counseling Psychology and Welfare Reform," *The Counseling Psychologist Vol. 27, no. 2: 263-284.*

*Hagen, Jan L.; Lurie, Irene (June 1993). "The Job Opportunities and Basic Skills Training Program and Child Care: Initial State Developments". <u>Social Service Review</u>. **67** (2): 198–216.*

Mattessich, Paul. (1992). "Collaboration-What Makes it Work: A Review of Review Literature on Factors Influencing Successful Collaboration," St. Paul: Amherst H. Wilder Foundation).

Lasker Roz D. and Weiss, Elisa S. (March 2003). "Broadening Participation in Community Problem Solving: a Multidisciplinary Model to Support Collaborative Practice and Research"

Journal of Urban Health: Bulletin of the New York Academy of Medicine. Vol. 80, No. 1, The New York Academy of Medicine.

Moffit, Robert A. and Ver Ploeg, Michele (Eds). (1999). "Evaluating Welfare Reform: A Framework and Review of Current Work," National Academy Press, Washington, D.C.

Office of Responsible Conduct of Research. (2005). Faculty Development and Instructional Design Center, Northern Illinois University.

Polit, Denise, Andrew London and John Martinez (May 2001). *The Health of Poor Urban Women: Findings from the Project on Devolution and Urban Change,* Manpower Demonstration Research Corporation.

Reid, William J.; Smith, Audrey D. (September 1972). "AFDC Mothers View the Work Incentive Program". *Social Service Review*. **46** (3): 347–362.

Robert Wood Foundation (November 2010) "Interdisciplinary Collaboration Improves Safety, Quality of Care, Experts Say," RWF News.

http://www.rwjf.org/en/library/articles-and-news/2010/11/interdisciplinary-collaboration-improves-safety-quality-of-care-.html

U.S. General Accounting Office, *TANF Recipients with Impairments Less Likely to be Employed and More Likely to Receive Federal Supports*, (GAO-03-210), December 2002.

United States Senate Committee on Finance, National Association of Social Workers. *Welfare Reform: Building on Success*. Hearings *March 12, 2003, Washington, DC, 2003. Print.*

Wilson, Betsy. (September 2017). "The Lone Ranger is Dead: Success Today Demands Collaboration," *College and Research Libraries News* vol. 61, no. 8.

The Value of the TANF Case Manager

Abstract

This paper describes the collaborative partnership between the University of the District of Columbia and the local government's human services agency. The government entered into a partnership with the university to provide job skills training to District residents receiving Temporary Assistance for Needy Families (TANF) benefits. Through the collaboration, the government has been able to prepare individuals for employment and become self-sufficient.

Yolandra A. Plummer, PhD

The University has engaged faculty in interdisciplinary collaboration and professional development. This partnership provides a snapshot of the value of the university in serving both the residents of the District of Columbia and local government policymakers.

Yolandra A. Plummer, PhD

Yolandra Plummer, PhD, is an associate professor at the University of the District of Columbia (UDC) in the School of Business and Public Administration (SBPA), Department of Public Administration. She also serves as the Director of the SBPA's Institute of Human Services Delivery. Dr. Plummer also serves on the Executive Board of Quality Trust for Individuals with Disabilities. She previously served as the Chief of Staff at the Department on Disability Services (DDS).

Introduction

Most government programs cannot meet all the needs of all its population. In response, policymakers engage in collaboration to circumvent bureaucratic boundaries and red tape. Today's human service delivery system includes a number of human service agencies that operate independently of each other. Often, each agency works in silos and is unaware of whom the other is serving. At times, more than one agency may be competing for the same resources and duplicating services. This creates a system of fragmented services. The end result is an unmet need, that of a low-income family.

This fragmentation presents insurmountable barriers for participants with multiple needs (Edelman & Radlin, 1991). Increasingly government agencies are collaborating with colleges and universities to administer public services and goods. In particular, human service agencies collaborate with universities to promote self-sufficiency and offer a unified service delivery system. Local governments collaborate with local colleges and universities to develop programs to serve their target populations.

The University of the District of Columbia is a public, historically black college and university (HBCU) and land grant institution in the District of Columbia. The University's mission is to offer an affordable education and workplace learning opportunities. The University partners with the local human services agency to provide job skills training to individuals receiving Temporary Assistance for Needy Families (TANF) benefits.

This collaborative partnership is consistent with the university's mission and vision. The university seeks to establish pathways for matriculation from workforce development. The vision also seeks to align educational offerings to student interests and District of Columbia priorities.

This article will examine how one government jurisdiction collaborated with a local university to provide services to residents. The research will draw upon the literature that focuses on the infrastructure and systems to support collaboration between local governments and university from the academic perspective.

Background

The Personal Responsibility and Work Opportunity Reconciliation Act (PRWORA) of 1996 changed the nation's welfare system. The federal legislation (Public Law 104-193) was introduced by Representative Eugene Clay Shaw, Jr. (R-FL.22). President Bill Clinton signed the Act into law on August 22, 1996. The Personal Responsibility and Work Reconciliation Act replaced the Temporary Assistance for Needy Families (TANF) benefits program. The new legislation became effective on July 1, 1997. The legislation replaced Aid to Families with Dependent Children

(AFDC), the federal entitlement program for low-income families, with state administered block grants.

The federal entitlement program had been in effect since 1935. In 1997, the TANF Program replaced the Job Opportunities and Basic Skills (JOBS) training program of 1988. The TANF program was reauthorized in the Budget Deficit Reduction Act of 2005. The Job Opportunities and Basic Skills Training program (JOBS) was a welfare-to-work program created by the Family Support Act of 1988. he Family Support Act replaced the Work Incentive program (WIN) created by the Social Security Act Amendments of 1967 (Hagen and Lurie, 1993 and Reid and Smith, 1972). The Family Support Act put the program under titles IV-A and IV-F of the Social Security Act.

The Temporary Cash Assistance for Needy Families (TANF) is a benefit program that provides cash assistance to needy families with dependent children when available resources do not fully address the family's need. Program participants are prepared for independence through job skills training, work activities and employment.

The legislation pushed states to experiment by designing their own social welfare programs. Though the legislation imposed new requirements on the state use of federal welfare funds, each state was encouraged to independently configure their program (Moffitt and Ver Ploeg, 1999).

In order to qualify for the TANF program in the District of Columbia, an individual must be a resident of the District of Columbia, pregnant or responsible for a child under 19 years of age. Other qualifications may include being a U.S. national, citizen, legal alien, or permanent resident with a low or very low income and be either under-employed (working for very low wages), unemployed or about to become unemployed (D.C. Department of Human Services (DHS), Economic Security Administration (ESA), 2014). Approximately 17,000 District of Columbia residents receive TANF benefits (DC Action for Children, 2016).

The University of the District of Columbia is a public, historically black college and university (HBCU) and land grant institution in the District of Columbia. The University's mission is to offer an affordable education and workplace learning opportunities. The partnership is consistent with the university's mission and vision. The University seeks to establish pathways for matriculation from workforce development. The vision also seeks to align educational offerings to student interests and District of Columbia priorities.

Institutions of higher education have vested interests in building strong relationships with surrounding communities of their campuses. They do not have the option of relocating and are of necessity place-based anchors. While businesses and residents often flee urban areas, universities remain (Birch, Perry and Taylor, 2013). Leaders have called for "engaged colleges and universities." Such an institution systematically structures, rewards and encourages partnerships and collaborations. An engaged institution collaborates with communities, not only in the traditional sense of educating students and producing relevant research, but also by focusing on community partnerships and collaborations (Mattessich, 1992). The University's current partnership with the government of the District of Columbia demonstrates its commitment, as an anchor institution, to serving the residents of the District of Columbia. Furthermore, it is the beginning to developing future collaborative agreements to address the needs of targeted populations.

A Collaboration Formed

In the District of Columbia, the Government of the District of Columbia human service agency administers the TANF benefits program. In 1996, the Department of Human Services entered into an agreement with the University of the District of Columbia (UDC) School of Business and Public Administration (SBPA). The School of Business and Public Administration's Institute of Human Service Delivery administers the job skills training program for TANF customers. The purpose of the program is to engage and train District residents who were receiving benefits in order to become self-sufficient and employable.

The agreement outlines three key goals. The first is to create a job skills training program for 700 low-income residents receiving Temporary Assistance for Needy Families (TANF)-*formerly known as the Aid to Families of Dependent Children* (AFDC). Second, to provide technical assistance to the Department of Human Services (DHS), Economic Security Administration (ESA) staff. Finally, to sponsor an Annual Capacity Building and Technical Assistance symposium for DHS grantees and community-based partners.

The collaboration reflects a growing trend of government and municipalities partnering across campuses to create sustainable urban partnerships.

In the mid to late 1980s, the Department of Human Services (DHS) was the largest District agency. It operated the city's largest budget and employee population. The agency had oversight over the city's entire health and human services delivery system. At the time, this included childcare, adult education, health care, welfare reform, elder care and other public services.

The demand for expanded capacity and greater efficiency led to the restructuring of the agency. The human services agency now primarily focuses on the human service delivery system for residents.

Since 1996, the Institute of Human Service Delivery has been working to improve the well-being of low-income individuals and families in the District of Columbia. The center is a component of the University of the District of Columbia (UDC) School of Business and Public Administration (SBPA). The center is located within the university's School of Business and Public Administration. The Institute's programs serve District residents who receive Temporary Assistance for Needy Families (TANF) benefits under the state TANF block grant.

The Institute, along with six other community-based providers, serves as TANF Employment Program (TEP) providers. The Institute offers two programs for residents receiving TANF benefits. The first program is the Paving Access Trails to Higher Security (PATHS). This program provides life skills training, job search and readiness training, vocational assessments, transportation assistance and job skills training. The job skills training includes certified nursing assistant (CNA), home health aide (HHA), hospitality, computer skills training, entrepreneurship and child development associate (CDA).

The second program, Program on Work, Employment and Responsibility (POWER), is for individuals receiving TANF benefits as well. The POWER Program offers specialized services and resources to DC residents with disabilities who are receiving TANF benefits.

Individuals who are in the POWER program are exempt from work participation requirements (but must comply with their self-sufficiency plan). Customers in the POWER program are exemption from the 60-month TANF time limit. The amount of a customer's cash assistance to the benefit amount received before any reductions (in the event, the customer, has exceeded the 60-month TANF time limit). The POWER program team engages customers through health and wellness promotion activities. The team also assists customers with obtaining Social Security Income. The University of the District of Columbia (UDC) team helps offer these services. The Institute also provides professional development training for local government staff and representatives of community-based grantee organizations. The Institute's programs promote workforce development, life skills training and health education at the community level.

Collaboration Begins at Home

Both the District of Columbia and University have mutually benefitted from the partnership. Together, both entities were able to create effective solutions to community needs, expand implement best practices and increase the understanding of human service delivery systems in urban settings. The University offers an environment whereby, both faculty and students, to foster an ethic of service and civic participation. Faculty and students gain experiential learning and professional development training.

This partnership is an opportunity for the University to examine its ability to identify and support new partnerships. The funding for university partnerships is important because of: 1) It can provide initial funding for programs and potentially attract funding from other sources in the future and 2) enable universities to develop and sustain an effective infrastructure and/or conducive environment to engage with communities (Ashenden et al., 2011).

The resources required to create the 'infrastructure' to support the program may be overlooked. The Institute is a single partnership. A significant proportion of these costs are for academic and administrative support staff time, although there may also be marketing and promotion costs as well as general office-related overheads. Faculty and staff are paid additional pay during the summer to perform work with the program. The Institute provides two computer labs, contracts with vendors to provide direct services and pays educational and examination fees. Additional costs include marketing and promotional materials for training, workshops and conferences, uniforms and other related costs for the program participants

If a University seeks status as an engaged institution-an institution that through its place-based relations strengthens its role as an urban anchor institution-then this must be registered in the institution's fiscal and structural investment in the process (Birch, Perry, Taylor, 2013).

The physical geographical location of the University has promoted intra university collaboration also has a geographical dimension. The majority of the services for program participants are offered at the University's main campus. The Institute provides the majority of its core services onsite at the university. This includes case management, job search and readiness training, intake and assessment, transportation assistance, child care referrals, health care coordination, mental health screenings and job skills trainings.

Ancillary supports services, such as vocational assessments, health and wellness support groups, life skills training, job search and readiness are offered at the main campus as well. Coordination of these services are centralized and managed through the SBPA Institute. A few of the job skill training classes are offered one of the University's other campus locations. One of the most unique features of this initiative has been its ability to utilize intra university collaboration. The across-university collaboration has been effective in improving the sustainability of the program because the majority of the services are offered at one location. Key questions for the program point to whether intra university collaboration will continue to yield benefits to the university-government partnership, enhance the support mechanisms for the program and influence the likely sustainability of support mechanisms and partnerships.

Universities are increasingly supportive of focusing on collaboration between researchers who offer different and complementary perspectives, knowledge, experience and skills that can result in innovative approaches to problem solving (Office of Responsible Conduct of Research, 2005). The program currently participates in intra university collaborations with the Departments of Social Work, Counseling and Psychology and Nursing.

Social Work

Since the beginning of welfare reform, the National Association of Social Workers (NASW) have supported PRWORA. The organization's core values include social justice and belief in the dignity and worth of each person. The organization's members maintain that the TANF program must accommodate the needs of all families, particularly those with disabilities.

According to the National Association of Social Workers, there is a distinct lack of awareness regarding the high percentage of families on TANF that are coping with disabling conditions. The most common disabilities for TANF beneficiaries include physical or mental health problems, drug and alcohol addictions, developmental disabilities and responsibility for the care of a disabled family member. Many are coping with one or more chronic conditions.

The General Accounting Office (GAO) found that at least 44 percent of TANF customers have physical or mental impairments or are caring for a child with impairments, compared with 15 percent of the non-TANF population (2002). Figures around 50 percent, both higher and lower, have been confirmed by the U.S. Department of Health and Human Services' Inspector General, as well as The Urban Institute, the Manpower Demonstration Research Corporation (MDRC) and others.

The Institute's program enlists the assistance of the University's licensed social workers and clinicians to conduct mental health and vocational assessments. The clinicians conduct screening and assessment procedures. These tools help identify the family's barriers and steps needed to assist them with obtaining greater independence.

The Institute employs Case Managers to advocate and guide the program participants. With the advent of the 1996 welfare reforms, the roles and responsibilities of the job changed dramatically. Case Managers hired prior to 1996 to work on the front lines in human services were trained to assess participant eligibility by processing them to determine their income and expenses, according to Cynthia Woodside, senior government relations associate at the NASW.

According to Woodside, "They were no longer just checking to determine whether someone was eligible for the program, but were really charged with screening for barriers, helping people find jobs and being a job coach once they found one." She adds "The workforce was not sufficiently trained to take on these responsibilities, and they recognized this fact." Many of the Institute's Case Managers were not prepared for the challenges of serving the TANF population.

The University's faculty in the Department of Social Work provided training for frontline staff on how to identify the basic signs and symptoms of the more common mental health disorders and substance abuse problems. If problems were identified, then one of the University's clinician's would provide a more in-depth assessment. Ensuring a qualified, stable and professional TANF workforce is a critical component of the program. Following enactment of the PRWORA, employees whose primary task had been to determine client eligibility was suddenly called upon to conduct customer assessments, engage customers in job search and job readiness training and placement activities, make referrals to related programs and special services and track customer activities. Many states have not invested sufficiently in the training needed to prepare their Case Managers for these additional tasks, nor have they hired more highly skilled staff.

Social workers are trained professionals who have bachelors, masters, or doctoral degrees in social work from an accredited social work program. In contrast, the majority of Case Managers today have little to no professional social work training. Case Managers often possess college degrees, but typically in fields unrelated to social service delivery. Some states only require Case Managers to have a high school diploma. Case Managers with the Institute possess a Masters degree along with at least one year of professional case management experience. They receive continuous training. This includes, but not limited to, mandated reporter writing, case management documentation, SSI/SSDI Outreach, Access and Recovery (SOAR), screen co-occurring disorders, non-crisis prevention intervention and domestic violence.

The ultimate success of welfare reauthorization depends, in large part, on the skills and abilities of the TANF workforce to implement the policies, it is critical that resources be directed to address current shortcomings.

Counseling and Psychology

The transition from welfare to work poses challenges. Individuals may face mental health issues and/or contextual variables (i.e., lack of a well-paying job). The Institute engages both Department of Counseling and Psychology faculty and students as consultants and interns. Faculty provide vocational guidance and psychological testing. The faculty maintains strong relationships with local mental health agencies and organizations in an effort to serve the needs of the Institute's participants.

Collaboration is drawn from many fields.,including social work, public adminsitration and sociology and others (Lasker and Weiss, 2003). Licensed clinicians and graduate students conduct vocational assessments and provide vocational guidance to participants seeking to transition from welfare to work.

Nursing

University nurse faculty conduct training workshops for the Institute's Case Managers. This includes reviewing medical records, developing comprehensive and coordinated physical and health care plans and record keeping. Specifically, the nurses demonstrate how to develop medical summary sheets for customer records. Case Managers are also trained on how to document and report health barriers in the centralized reporting system. Nurse faculty also receive continuous education units (CEUs) for training and use them as a part of their professional portfolios.

Collaborative Education begins Early

The Institute offers internships to a broad mix of students enrolled in the Counseling and Psychology, Public Administration, Social Work and Computer Information Systems. The program includes students from other universities in the metropolitan area as well. Students must begin working together before they actually start working. Students participate in a year-long internships and collaborate with Case Managers in the development of each participant's development plan. Students gain from the experiences and learn to distinguish and differentiate certain conditions (i.e., depression, anxiety) from poorly defined vocational interests and lack of job-related self-efficacy (Edwards, et. al, 1999).

Students are taught consultation, program development and program evaluation skills through work with social service agencies. The provision of such experiences will likely advance the training agenda of the field (Edwards et. al, 1999).

Many professionals operate in silos. It is incumbent upon universities and training programs to expand interdisciplinary educational opportunities and programs to help foster collaboration among students before they enter the workforce (Robert Wood Foundation, 2010). Interdisciplinary collaboration can provide people with many learning experiences, but only if they are properly managed (Chu, 2013).

Lessons Learned

Through the collaboration, the University has trained more than 10,000 District residents receiving TANF benefits and prepared them to work in hospitality and health careers. The University has opened and shared its core facilities with government officials. Through the Institute, the University has provided onsite leadership, sponsored and conference for more than 15 community-based organizations on an annual basis and continuously developed professional development workshops training for the human services front line staff.

Furthermore, the University has hired five of its interns who remain as current employees, formed community partnerships and increased its grant funding from the government. This has increased the visibility of the program and confidence of the District government in the University's ability to provide and sustain city programs.

There are scholars who are cautious about interdisciplinary collaborations in the academic setting. For some, concerns included credit for publishing (Chu, 2013). Others maintain that the focus on interdisciplinary research distracts one from their primary field of study.

As the District government policymakers juggle competing priorities and dwindling budgets, they must evaluate the value of university partnerships. Universities can share training and technological resources with government to reduce their agency cost. Both entities share common interests and objectives in serving the District of Columbia. Moving forward, both entities must evaluate innovative approaches to service delivery, including best practices to promote government and university collaboration.

Works Cited

"The Engaged University," (Spring /Summer 1998). *Penn State Outreach* 1, no. 1

Ashenden, Stuart, Hoult, Elizabeth, Matthews, Nairne, Bruce, Steve and Pratt, Jonathan. (2011). Collaboration between Universities: An Effective Way of Sustaining Community University Partnerships?" *Gateways: International Journal of Community Research and Engagement Vol 4: 119–35.*

Birch, Perry and Taylor, 2013. "Universities as Anchor Institutions," *Journal of Higher Education Outreach and Engagement*, v. 17, no. 3. 7-15.

Chu. Andrea. (2013). "Interdisciplinary Collaboration at the University Level," Honors Research Thesis. Ohio State University: School of Environment and Natural Resources.

Edwards, Scott, Rachal, Chris and Dixon David N. (1999). "Counseling Psychology and Welfare Reform," *The Counseling Psychologist Vol. 27, no. 2: 263-284.*

Hagen, Jan L.; Lurie, Irene (June 1993). "The Job Opportunities and Basic Skills Training Program and Child Care: Initial State Developments". Social Service Review. 67 (2): 198–216.

Mattessich, Paul. (1992). "Collaboration-What Makes it Work: A Review of Review Literature on Factors Influencing Successful Collaboration," St. Paul: Amherst H. Wilder Foundation).

Lasker Roz D. and Weiss, Elisa S. (March 2003). "Broadening Participation in Community Problem Solving: a Multidisciplinary Model to Support Collaborative Practice and Research"

Journal of Urban Health: Bulletin of the New York Academy of Medicine. Vol. 80, No. 1, The New York Academy of Medicine.

Moffit, Robert A. and Ver Ploeg, Michele (Eds). (1999). "Evaluating Welfare Reform: A Framework and Review of Current Work," National Academy Press, Washington, D.C.

Office of Responsible Conduct of Research. (2005). Faculty Development and Instructional Design Center, Northern Illinois University.

Polit, Denise, Andrew London and John Martinez (May 2001). *The Health of Poor Urban Women: Findings from the Project on Devolution and Urban Change,* Manpower Demonstration Research Corporation.

Reid, William J.; Smith, Audrey D. (September 1972). "AFDC Mothers View the Work Incentive Program". *Social Service Review*. **46** (3): 347–362.

Robert Wood Foundation (November 2010) "Interdisciplinary Collaboration Improves Safety, Quality of Care, Experts Say," RWF News.

http://www.rwjf.org/en/library/articles-and-news/2010/11/interdisciplinary-collaboration-improves-safety-quality-of-care-.html

U.S. General Accounting Office, *TANF Recipients with Impairments Less Likely to be Employed and More Likely to Receive Federal Supports*, (GAO-03-210), December 2002.

United States Senate Committee on Finance, National Association of Social Workers. *Welfare Reform: Building on Success*. Hearings *March 12, 2003, Washington, DC, 2003. Print.*

Wilson, Betsy. (September 2017). "The Lone Ranger is Dead: Success Today Demands Collaboration," *College and Research Libraries News* vol. 61, no. 8.

The Value of the TANF
Case Manager

Case Managers in human service delivery systems serve as the key point of contact for the individuals on their caseload. These Case Managers serve individuals with an array of barriers and challenges in obliging individuals who receive Temporary Assistance for Needy Families (TANF) benefits.

The Temporary Assistance for Needy Families (TANF) program is designed to help needy families achieve self-sufficiency. States receive block grants to design and operate programs that accomplish one of the purposes of the TANF program. The four purposes of the TANF program are to:

- Assist needy families so that children can be cared for in their own homes
- Reduce the dependency of needy parents by promoting job preparation, employment and marriage stability
- Prevent and reduce the incidence of out-of-wedlock pregnancies
- Encourage the formation and maintenance of two-parent families (U.S. Department of Health and Human Services (DHHS), 2017)

The roles of Case Managers are multifaceted. Their primary role is to assist an individual and/or a family to become self-supporting while evaluating all the basic needs. This is initially performed through a comprehensive assessment of the individual's needs and development of an Individual Responsibility Plan (IRP).

According to the National Association of Social Workers, case management is both macro and micro in nature (NASW, 1992). The Case Manager intervenes on both the customer and system level to determine the best needs for the customer and how those needs fit into the state system (NASW, 1992).

The Case Manager coordinates needed services to help an individual obtain services in the service delivery system. The face-to-face evaluation gauges the individual's strengths and weaknesses. It helps the Case Manager to identify and outline goals and maximize the well-being of the individual and in some cases the entire family. Then, the Case Manager coordinates the appropriate state services and benefits.

Benefit delivery is integrated with self-sufficiency-enhancing services. Depending on an individual's needs, the Case Manager may coordinate services and/or benefits to include the following services: housing, childcare, food and nutrition, medical benefits, mental health, domestic violence, substance abuse support, disability (i.e., intellectual and/or developmental and learning) and any other condition that may pose a barrier for an individual.

The Case Manager who serves customers receiving Temporary Assistance for Needy Families (TANF) has the primary responsibility for determining that an individual may have documented and hidden barriers to employment. The Case Manager conducts a preliminary assessment in order to develop an IRP for the customer and identify barriers.

The Case Manager refers an individual to a partner agency for services to address and/or remove a barrier. Case Managers are responsible for helping individuals understand their conditions and recommend actions for barrier removal. Once an action plan or individual responsibility plan is established, the Case Manager monitors to ensure the individual's compliance with their service plan. This will also demonstrate any progress toward achieving self-sufficiency.

Roles Change: Pre-TANF, Case Managers primarily performed intake and benefits determination. The TANF program approach focuses on case management. The approach focuses on job skills training and employment. The social services program focuses on addressing personal (including medical, childcare, transportation, domestic violence, substance abuse and employment training.) and family (including childcare, housing, child abuse and housing) issues that interfere with seeking and obtaining employment.

The TANF program provides a different set of regulations for individuals with documented physical and mental health condition and other medical conditions. Individuals who have obtained a medical certification of a mental health condition, are pregnant and/or caring for a family, are removed from a Case Manager's general caseload. The specific state program requirements for this population vary. Individuals who meet the specific program requirement**s are** exempted from employment activities.

Identification of hidden barriers is a new role for many Case Managers. Post TANF, the roles of TANF Case Manager's changed to include the identification and mitigation of personal and employment roadblock to employment.

It is important for a TANF Case Manager to develop, maintain and strengthen partnerships with other agency and service provider staff. These individuals are critical in assisting the Case Manager to obtain the services for barrier removal for the customer. Staff in other agencies can provide information, assistance, and support to the customer.

This is especially important for individuals who have a hidden and/or documented barrier. A study found that a TANF Case Manager is the individual who identifies that an individual has hidden barriers (Thompson, Van Ness and O'Brien, 2001). TANF Case Managers play an integral role in initial barrier identification efforts.

A Case Manager's abilities to fulfill barrier identification responsibilities are affected by their other responsibilities, skills, training and the size of their caseloads. Not every Case Manager is experienced and/or skillfully trained to identify and/or document hidden barriers. The ability to detect an individual's hidden barriers highlights a key competency of a TANF Case Manager. Individuals with hidden barriers tend to remain on an individual's caseload longer and are challenging in every way.

There are key competencies that are valuable when recruiting for a TANF Case Manager. In competency modeling, the intent is not to focus how a role has been performed to date, but rather to identify the behaviors that will be needed to achieve long-term strategic goals. In this sense, competency modeling is forward looking and not rooted in the past (Korn Ferry, 2017).

The advantage of using competencies is that they are measurable skills, attitudes, or attributes that can be closely aligned to organizational strategy. Examples of competencies include business acumen, patience, perspective, and planning (Korn Ferry, 2017).

Key competencies found in TANF Case Managers include accountability, patience, collaboration, patience, flexibility, communication, professional development and training, advocacy, interpersonal skills, communication, empathy and resourceful.

Accountability

There must be an individual TANF Case Manager in place for case management to be successful. This individual must maintain oversight of the human services delivery system for the whole care process. This includes the array of services that an individual will access and need to move towards self-sufficiency. There is a risk of fragmentation in the human services delivery system when a Case Manager is not accountable or has not been assigned to an individual.

Patience The role of a TANF Case Manager is an intensive case management type. It requires the use of patience with individuals who face complex barriers. Patience is needed when serving individuals who face barriers to employment and are seeking to maximize their well-being. Patience is important because individuals may be noncompliant with meeting the goals of their individual service plan. The Case Manager conducts face-to-face exchanges with individuals and intervenes with individuals who may not be compliant with their service plan. Individuals may have a history of lateness and/or missed appointments. Difficulty with facing other barriers may impact an individual's ability to meet their previously scheduled appointments and/or deadlines with their Case Manager.

Collaboration Case management is largely shaped by working with other agencies and service providers to coordinate care and share information. Systems and crisis theory awareness allows for decision making that is sufficiently global to protect all entities involved in case management. It is more about the ability to tune in to an organization's informal patterns of collaboration; it will be less about having specific skills and more about having the essential qualities that foster collaboration itself — empathy, emotional intelligence, diplomacy and negotiation. The outcome of case management is increased individual and family stability and self-sufficiency through individualized case management.

Case management requires team effort. Collaboration is enhanced when the entire team is in harmony. The team consists of the individual (family), Case Manager and community partners with whom the individual may be working. The individuals served by TANF Case Manager often receive services from multiple agencies and organizations. This requires coordination and collaboration with other agencies between the TANF Case Manager and agency staff.

Multi-agency collaboration is becoming increasingly relevant to policymakers and practitioners (Rose, 2007). TANF Case Managers develop relationships with staff at other state agencies and community-based organizations to coordinate services for individuals on their caseload.

An individual's expertise and attitudes, from previous experiences of multi-agency working, is critical to collaboration with other agencies. (Cameron and Lart, 2003; Sloper, 2004).

Working together towards a common goal raises issues for professionals from different agencies and backgrounds. Such difficulties stem partially from differing ideologies, working practices and priorities (Rose, 2007). The coordination and sharing of information among the variety of staff and partners involved in identifying and addressing barriers is complicated and requires a significant investment in communication and collaboration at multiple levels (Thompson, Van Ness and O'Brien. 2001).

Flexibility

Flexibility is an openness to different and new ways of doing things. It is a willingness to modify one's preferred way of doing things (Cripe and Mansfield, 2002). Flexibility means more than adjustments in a Case Manager's schedule. It requires the TANF Case Manager to change their mindset to see the merits of perspectives of others.

The TANF Case Manager must be prepared for any change in the individual's condition at any given. The Case Manager must be ready with a solution or temporary answer. For example, a Case Manager maybe required to search the streets in order to reach them an individual, become displaced and find a new residence within 24 hours. The TANF Case Manager must be able to respond immediately with a resolution no matter their geographic location or time of day.

Managing Change

TANF Case Managers continuously manage change. In response, they help and guide the individuals on their caseload to manage any change that directly affects the individual and/or their family. William Bridges proposes a transition model to guide individuals through change. Under his model, he proposes to focus on transition not change (Bridges, 1991).

Bridges maintains that change happens to all people. "Transition is internal. It is what happens in people's minds as they experience change," says Bridges.

There are three stages in the Transition model. The three stages include Ending, Losing and Letting Go, Neutral Zone and A New Beginning. Individuals progress through each stage at their own progress. Case Managers can use the model to understand how an individual is feeling at each stage. Initially, it is important to listen emphatically and communicate openly with individuals.

Communication

Individual Level

Communicating effectively is an important competency for the TANF Case Manager. Individuals may complain about not being able to reach their Case Manager. The TANF Case Manager must develop strong lines of communication with the individuals whom they serve and work. This means the individuals on their caseload as well as team members are able to reach them via mail, telephone and/or face-to-face meetings. Regular communication is the cornerstone to helping an individual to achieve their self-sufficiency goals.

In instances where individuals are transient and/or there is a loss of contact (unreported change of address or interruption in telephone service), the TANF Case Manager must be quick on their feet. The savvy TANF Case Manager will integrate the use of technology as an avenue to communicate with individuals on their caseload. The Case Manager will frequently monitor social media (Twitter, Facebook and Snapchat) to track, communicate and fully engage with individuals.

Agency Level

At an agency level, the TANF Case Manager must be able to communicate with all providers in the human services delivery system that provide services for individuals on their caseload. The range of services received and individual progress must be documented by the Case Manager. This information must also be communicated verbally when soliciting for assistance for an individual.

Education and Professional Development and Training

The right set of skills is just as important as a Case Manager being able to access the appropriate training, support and mentors in place. According to Sharon Mass, current president of the American Case Management Association (ACMA), "formal education (Bachelors and Masters) sets a standard whereby people learn critical thinking skills. One must be a clear communicator and possess an awareness of regulations." She adds that Case Managers are patient advocates that must be aware of the rules and regulations.

Many Case Managers are now required to obtain a mandated reporter training certification and participate in non-crisis violent prevention training. Mandated reporters are individuals who have regular contact with vulnerable people, such as individuals receiving TANF benefits. They are legally required to ensure a report is made when abuse is observed or suspected. Specific details vary across jurisdictions. The abuse that must be reported may include neglect, or financial, physical, sexual or other types of abuse.

Non-crisis violent prevention training emphasizes early intervention techniques for preventing or managing disruptive behavior. Personal safety techniques and restraint and transport techniques

Advocacy/Job Coach (empower)

Moss emphasizes the importance of empowering individuals to prepare for their future needs. A TANF Case Manager is able to empower individuals by recognizing they are capable, have strengths and resources that can help individuals take control of their lives. Case Managers treat individuals respectfully, assisting them in identifying their needs, building on their strengths while supporting them in meeting their goals.

A major component of case management is advocating for individuals. This involves coordinating with various professionals or teams and negotiating with them to secure medication, equipment and support services. It is important for the Case Manager to have some influence over service providers (Webb, 2013).

Interpersonal Skills

In a study conducted with welfare recipients about their Case Manager performance, substantive competence, accessibility and interpersonal skills were noted as three key dimensions (Anderson, 2001). From the perspective of an individual receiving TANF benefits, a Case Manager with strong interpersonal skills makes them feel like someone is "looking out for them."

Empathy

It is essential that Case Managers are able to develop good relationships and communicate with a range of people. They need to be approachable and able to demonstrate empathy, even when addressing apparently 'minor concerns.'

Resourceful

A TANF Case Manager is a broker of information. They are what Robert Germane coins "central connectors" and "brokers" of information flow (Germane, 2012). Case Managers often think of themselves as 'fixers.' They find solutions to problems by drawing on various service providers and informal care networks, if available. A lack of access to information and resources and a lack of stakeholder support have been identified as barriers to effective case management. It can occasionally fall on case management staff to work autonomously in overcoming these difficulties. In an environment of limited resources. Case Managers find themselves always seek resources for their customers.

Being a Case Manager allows an individual the ability to see a bigger picture of the individual and the human services delivery system. There are challenges. According to Christy Whetsell, President-Elect of the American Case Management Association (ACMA), "You will find that no two days are alike. It's the feeling of doing what's right for the individual and smile of relief from the individual that keeps you returning back to do it again the next day."

The formal study of TANF Case Management is still in its infancy. Case Managers and their customers learn more new things about case management everyday. Just like no two days are alike, no two Case Managers are the same. There are Case Managers who are firm and less forgiving while others make repeated requests without consequences.

Case Managers wear various hats including being motivational speakers, counselors, confidants and mentors to some extent.

There is much to be examined and learned about the value of a TANF Case Manager. The TANF Case Manager plays substantial roles in improving the well-being of individuals seeking to become self-sufficient. They are living examples and role models to the individuals whom they serve whether they accept this added responsibility or not.

Future efforts should focus on continuous training and support for TANF Case Managers. Training will guide Case Managers in recognizing and documenting the challenges customers face. This includes making referrals to partner agencies and seeking out new resources in a system of limited funds. Furthermore, many states can better support their frontline employees by expanding support for TANF Case Managers.

About the Author

Yolandra A. Plummer, PhD is an Associate Professor at the University of the District of Columbia who has served as the Principal Investigator of a grant for seven years to provide work readiness training for some of the most vulnerable residents in the District of Columbia.